M000169585

Skira Architecture Library

Luca Molinari

Santiago Calatrava

Catalogue entries by
Erika Samsa

Photographs of completed works by
Paolo Rosselli

Skira

Graphic design and cover
Pierluigi Cerri
with Dario Zannier

Research and indices
Erika Samsa

Copy editing
Antonio Scarfoglio
Emanuela Chiesa

Layout
Paola Ranzini

Translations
Jeff Jennings

Photography
Sergio Belinchon
Alessandra Chemollo
Heinrich Helfenstein
Paolo Rosselli

First published in Italy in
1998

© 1999 by Skira, Milan
All rights reserved under
international copyright
conventions.

No part of this book may
be reproduced or utilized
in any form or by any
means, electronic or
mechanical, including
photocopying, recording,
or any information storage
and retrieval system,
without permission in
writing from the publisher.

Printed and bound in Italy.
First edition

Distributed in North
America and Latin
America by Abbeville
Publishing Group, 22
Cortlandt Street, New
York, NY 10007, USA..
Distributed elsewhere in
the world by Thames and
Hudson Ltd., 181a High
Holborn, London WC1V
7QX, United Kingdom.

ISBN 88-8118-525-3

Table of Contents

Luca Molinari

The "Case" of Santiago Calatrava

8

With more than ten years having passed since Pierluigi Nicolin published the essay that introduced the "Calatrava case" into the international debate, it remains as relevant as ever to ask the same questions posed back then regarding an artistic personality and an architectural *oeuvre* that can still be defined as "quite unexpected [...] and without any immediately recognizable, easily verifiable sources or counterparts"[1].

In this past decade the architect-engineer from Valencia has sustained a level of productivity that is, to say the least, furious: 190 projects, approximately 55 of which have been built or are under construction. And with those projects, he has established himself as one of the most highly controversial figures in a field that tends for the most part toward a tired and tiresome ecumenism.

The radicality of the positions assumed by both the critical community and the general public compels us inevitably to investigate a phenomenon that intersects with at least three disparate but related issues: the redefinition of the relationship between architecture and engineering, the crisis of the professions and their social credibility, and the difficulty faced by critics in devising a language that would allow them to interpret heterodox phenomena. To this we might add the uniqueness of Calatrava's "intellectual biography", which helps us understand, in part anyway, the otherwise incomprehensible panoply of interests and conceptual tools that he has assembled since taking degrees in architecture (Valencia) and engineering (Zurich's ETH), since his youthful apprenticeship at an arts and trade school, since having embraced the study of anatomy and descriptive and dynamic geometry, passions which he has obsessively pursued over the years[2].

In an historical period that tends ever more toward hyper-specialization and the fragmentation of knowledge, Calatrava manifests an interdisciplinary breadth and professional versatility that is truly awesome. But apart from the remarkableness of the individual in question, this situation emphasizes the necessity of examining the still problematic relationship between university training, predominant cognitive models, and the evolution of contemporary technology and building methods.

Study sketches for the transept of the Cathedral of St. John in New York

The frequent accusations of "formalism" become a moot point when we consider that they derive from the theoretical and technical limitations of a functionalist approach incapable of unburdening itself of the heavy yoke of its own founding principles, or of establishing linguistic and interpretive parameters capable of dealing with an alternative architecture. Indeed, the strength of Calatrava's work lies in his having demonstrated how analogical and imaginative thought can be joined with specialized technical knowledge to create a new and different formal and spatial language with a powerful symbolic charge.

His working method, as he himself often points out, is a species of experimentalism wherein design is deliberately problematized to the point where it becomes selfsame as artistic research, thus opening up interesting new perspectives from which to address the complexity of

[1] P. Nicolin, *Deduzione-induzione-abduzione*, in *Santiago Calatrava. Il folle volo*, Electa, Milan 1987, p. 9

[2] S. Calatrava, *Disertacionaes*, in "El Croquis", no. 38, Madrid 1989, pp. 4-11

[3] "The events of the mid-1960s and early 1970s eroded the confidence of the public, and of the professionals themselves, that are existed an armamentarium of theories and techniques sufficient to remove the troubles that beset society. [...] The crises of confidence in the professions, and perhaps also the decline in professional self-image, seems to be rooted in a growing skepticism about professional effectiveness in the larger sense, a skeptical reassessment of the professions' actual contribution to society's well being through the delivery of competent services based on special knowledge", in Donald A. Schon, *The reflective practitioner*, Basic Books, 1983, pp. 11-13.

[4] "The equation of the beautiful and the moral is one of the leit-motifs of many architects of our epoch, of those spirits most sensitive to ethical problems like Mies van der Rohe, who loved to repeat St. Augustine's dictum, 'Beauty is the splendor of the Truth'", E. Nathan Rogers, *Personalità di Pier Luigi Nervi*, in *Pier Luigi Nervi*, Ed. Comunità, Milan 1962, p. XI.

contemporary reality, not through a rigid typological schematism but through the creation of *exemplary constructions* capable of functioning as recognizable territorial signs.

And it is in fact on the problem of social "recognition", and on the identity of contemporary architecture and engineering in particular, that the projects of the Valencian artist seem to play.

Much of the architecture of this century has been conceived in the throes of the dilemma between the desire to rebuild society by annihilating existing visual and material culture and the secret, desperate need for the "real world's" acceptance of the Modernist esthetic.

The widening of the rupture in modern culture between the social body and the symbolic recognizability of the art object or public space is signalled on the one hand by the progressive fragmentation and incommunicability between their respective languages (think of all the parodies of modern art, from Hogarth to Loos' manhole cover to Alberto Sordi's spoof of the Venice Biennial), and on the other by society's definitive withdrawal of faith in the thaumaturgic powers of professional technical knowledge[3]. At the same time, the illusory modernist axiom that equated an object's beauty with its morality[4], that decree of an ethics of technology and its potential to save the world, has been progressively discredited in the face of the relativization of the content of modernist culture and the environmental crisis that has devastated our planet over the past few decades. The role of contemporary architecture and engineering has emerged from this scenario so diminished in importance as to find itself relegated to a matter of mere taste and custom, overwhelmed by a voracious, media-dominated artistic culture, relinquishing in many countries its once determinant role in the construction of the human environment.

The polemical controversy surrounding Calatrava's work, comparable to that provoked by a only a handful of other contemporary architects (eg. the bitter debate over the Eisenman-Serra monument in Berlin, the international uproar that accompanies every work by Gehry or Libeskind), immediately draws our attention to the impasse at which much of the architectural community presently finds itself, and at the same time emphasizes the difficulty of transcending the traditionally rigid separation of architecture and engineering by way of an approach that might be defined, among other things, as artistic.

9

Twisting Torso, 1993

This point raises two other problems against which 20th century culture seems to have regularly run aground: that of the relationship between individual creativity, the artistic status of its expression and the collective vision of the modern; and consequently, that of the role of decoration in modern architecture.

If on the one hand the postwar period definitively buried the illusory pretence of the annulment of individual artistic personality at the hands of a theoretical absolutism, the debate over the relationship between decoration and structure, which has never really been articulated, has become far more heated and contradictory.

Many of the accusations aimed at Calatrava's work, whether because of the excessive dimensions of a given construction or its linguistic excess in justifying its own simplicity and *truth*, seem to indicate the persistence of an age-old theoretical misunderstanding.

Behind the Calvinistic hypocrisy of seeing ornament as sin hides what has become the *horror vacui* of our turn-of-the-millenium culture, which manifests itself in the difficulty of acknowledging the possibility of an architecture that is *also* the free artistic expression of form, be it natural or mathematical.

Meanwhile, the visionary charge of some of Calatrava's more recent projects, from the Auditorium in Tenerife to the City of Science in Valencia to the Milwaukee Museum of Art, seems to forcefully underscore his intention to proceed, heedless of criticism, along his chosen path of investigating the forms of architecture and their visual and communicative potential.

Calatrava's masterful control of projective geometry, his technological experimentation, and his almost offhand use of complex building techniques all contribute to an intensification of the expressive power of his works, a high degree of seductiveness that operates on two levels: that of the structure's assertive territorial *presence* on the one hand, and that of its prioritization of the relationship between architecture and the user/viewer on the other.

With this second point in mind, it is important to note how the great works of engineering, even the more recent ones, have maintained a significant impact on the collective imagination, thanks to the demiurgic power that modern culture has always attributed to the machine, and how many of Calatrava's works demonstrate an keen awareness of this, positioning themselves in a direct line of ascent, as it were, with the masterpieces of the great modern engineers, from Paxton to Eiffel, from Maillart and Freyssenet to Nervi and Candela.

Calatrava shares with these masters what Ernesto Rogers defined as the power of the medium, who brings to material life "the phantasms of the laws of statics, which appear to others behind the ungraspable symbolism of numbers"[5]; warlocks in the guise of modern artists, capable of giving form to modernity's anxieties and new utopias alike. Unlike his ancestors and colleagues, however, our Catalan architect seems to have definitively overcome the precondition of the ethicality of technique, arriving at a greater awareness of the formal and perceptual qualities of the work.

A project executed at the ETH in 1979 and two of his first works provide the earliest testimony of this paradigmatic rejection, as well as revealing interesting connections with the Zurich architectural scene of the time. The subject of the ETH project: "*plastisches Gestalten*"; its demonstration: a portable pool, made from a sheet of transparent plastic just one millimeter thick, 24,000 liters of water suspended from the ceiling of the institute's great hall by a sophisticated system of cables; the image: a human being floating peacefully in the void.

Shadow Machine, 1994

The two works, both executed in collaboration with Bruno Reichlin and Fabio Reinhart: the unrealized project for the Iba Squash Hall (1979), and the Ernstings factory in Coesfeld (built 1983).

The first of these is a movable structure, a canopy for two squash courts whose motorized "wings" of copper-sheathed wood can assume different positions in response to use and weather conditions. A lightweight machine with a vague Leonardesque flavor, an "unexpected"[6] object, a dynamic element set within the reconstruction of the city block designed by the two Swiss students of Aldo Rossi.

The second project involves the reworking of the exterior of a large factory. Each of the four facades is treated with a different material and a different composition (this is one of the first instances of a building being clad in a variety of metal patterns, anticipating a practice that became widespread during the '90s). Yet there is an overarching classical order, in the form of a high basement and a delicate trabeation, that unites them.

The mechanized movement of the three central folding doors, along with the astonishment it provokes, are the variants that lie at the heart of the building's deliberately surprising image.

The articulated joint used for the door dates back to Calatrava's doctoral thesis ("On the Foldability of Frames", and would eventually be patented. But what is important to note here is how these earliest hands-on experiences with movable structures seems indirectly linked to a polytechnical dimension in which the continuity of modernist orthodoxy is overlapped by the disquieting theoretical and linguistic revisionism of Aldo Rossi.

But it would be reductive to see the sphere of influence as being limited to Zurich and Rossi, for in reality Calatrava's work draws from, and follows, a wide variety of sources and paths, which are often determined by the specific conditions of the project at hand, and invariably stimulated by his unceasing research into the forms of nature.

Testifying to that effect is the formidable series of bridges and pedestrian walkways designed and built over the past 15 years, the whole of which is regulated by a conception of the bridge as an ordering element of the territory it occupies, as a recognizable sign. It is never seen as the merely technical problem of joining one parcel of *terra firma* to another (engineering's originary gesture, its most ancient chal-

11

Detail of the folding doors of the Ernstings factory

"On the Foldability of Frames", doctoral thesis, ETH, Zurich, 1979

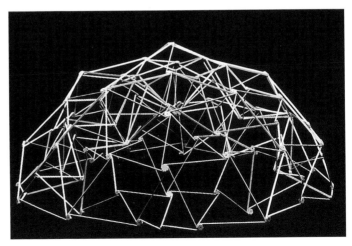

[5] *Ibid.*, p. X
[6] P. Nicolin, *op.cit.*, p. 10

lenge), but as the existential one of establishing a bridge's identity as *unicum*, an object whose role is as much a function of the biography of its builder as the context in which it is built.

The infinite variations to which Calatrava subjects the design of a bridge, always departing from the theme of an existing typology (arch, suspension, truss, bascule, swing, et. al.) bear witness to his incessant research. Technique itself is inevitably pushed to a critical extreme, crystallized in its own physical limit; likewise, the endowing of certain projects with the power of movement (the Médoc bridge in Bordeaux, the bridge for the Port of Barcelona) heightens the vertigo with which they are perceived.

The bridge embodies the modern metaphor of the body "without rest [...] continually traversed by movement"[7], the movement of people, vehicles, information, investments, ideas. The pretence that the bridge, or any product of engineering for that matter, should epitomize solidity, stability, material and mental security is radically challenged by a vision of architecture that seeks instead to reflect the complexity and transience of many of the cultural and economic processes that define today's civilization.

Calatrava invariably conceives his projects three-dimensionally – that is, in terms of section and elevation rather than plan – preferring to work with volumes rather than areas, and at the same time wanting to control the overall form of those volumes, their visual and emotional impact as objects in space.

The dominion of the "beauty"[8] of the section over a rigorous plan (which by no means suggests that Calatrava is inattentive to the latter) is combined with the concrete application of projective geometry which in recent years seems to be moving increasingly to the fore in the generative process of the project.

The powerful plasticity and visionary quality of the subterranean spaces of the Stadelhofen in Zurich finally reach the light of day in the Lyon-Satolas TGV station, and later in the Auditorium of Tenerife and Valencia's City of Science. As Calatrava is commissioned with ever larger and more complex projects, so does their geometry become more complex, and his work seems increasingly to express that state of "unfinished-ness"[9], so aptly described by Tzonis-Lefaivre,

12

[7] A. Tzonis, L. Lefaivre, *Movement structures and the work of Santiago Calatrava*, Birkhäuser, Basel-Berlin 1995, pp. 72-90.
[8] S. Calatrava, *op. cit.*, pp. 4-5.
[9] A. Tzonis, L. Lefaivre, *op. cit.*, pp. 118-123.

Stadelhofen Station, Zurich. Detail of the underground spaces

whereby their form appears to be the materialization of the conceptual processes that generated it.

The refined use of a variety of materials that the architect manifests, indeed almost flaunts in his earliest major works – the Stadelhofen and Lucerne railway stations, the high school in Wohlen, the bridges of Barcelona, Seville, Merida and Valencia – has been further intensified in recent years with the aim of giving yet greater expressive potential to the materials of architecture. This aim is clearly in keeping with an artistic research that has from the outset run side by side with design, as we see in the splendid Tenerife Exposition Center, where the vast sheet metal roof appears to balance on the reinforced concrete spine, its extremities just barely resting on the lateral structures clad in local stone. The numerous sketchbooks in which Calatrava documents the genesis and evolution of a given project, sometimes arriving as far as a fully developed scale drawing of a building module or assembly technique, testify to the intense interpenetration of artistic exploration, architectural design and engineering. Indeed, leafing through one of these sketchbooks, one encounters everything from broad thematic drawings to meticulously detailed watercolors to human figures to ideas for sculptures.

Stadelhofen Station, Zurich. The new structure in relation to the urban landscape

The works of these last few years indicate a progressive evolution of Calatrava's formal and linguistic research, and offer a glimpse into his ongoing quest to articulate the complexities and amplify the expressivity of his work. After the brilliant "surgical" interventions in Zurich and Lucerne, the large-scale territorial projects constitute an elaborate montage of certain of the architectural premises developed earlier; the glazed galleries, the spectacular roofs, and the mobile elements become components of a composition wherein biography and new solutions are combined to establish an as yet undefined architecture capable of resisting the anonymous density of the urban sprawl.

The monumental project for the City of Science, even more so than the expansion of the Milwaukee Museum of Art, exemplifies this quest, a quest characterized by a constant pursuit of plasticity, the expressive power of architectural forms, and the difficulty of combining them in the physical context of the contemporary metropolis, as well as in the cultural context of contemporary architectural values.

13

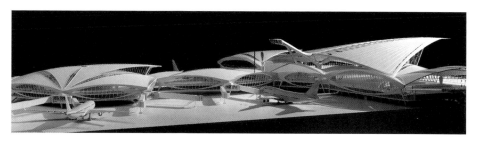

Barajas-Madrid Airport. Scale model

Early Works

The works that constitute Calatrava's debut on the international stage – those executed between 1979 and the commencement of work on the Zurich Stadelhofen in 1985 – reveal a heterogeneous vision in which the formal lexicon and operative approach that will characterize his architecture in the years to come are already clear and coherent.

His doctoral dissertation on "the pliability of structures in space", submitted to the ETH in Zurich in 1979, is essentially the outline of a poetics that hinges on three key points: the complex deployment of geometry, the achievement of structural lightness and formal dynamism through experimentation, and the power of an ambitious feat of engineering to astound.

Technological experimentation is not ostentatiously flaunted, however, but rather placed at the service of the formal result, an element of the overall composition.

While the plan is utilized in a classical way as a regulative system of spatial organization, the section is the motor of formal complexity, the element of "beauty" that invests the work with its own distinctive identity.

The theme of the roof, focal point of some of Calatrava's ear-

"Calatrava's structures are like moving vessels designed to contain the mobility of contemporary life, and seem to incorporate [that mobility] into the configurations of their forms.
The volumes preserve the memory of the processes that generate them; their genesis and evolution are inherent in their form."

(Alexander Tzonis, Liane Lefaivre, 1995)

liest experiments, exemplifies this process – one can trace the natural evolution of the sail motif, for example, from the competition entry for the Züspa-Zurich exposition complex to the Jakem factory to the Cabaret Tabourettli and the Bärenmatte community center.

During this same period, the project for another industrial building – the Ernstings factory, codesigned with Reichlin and Reinhart – offers the architect the possibility of addressing two other themes symbolically linked to his training in Zurich: the folding access doors concretize the experiments with movement and articulated joints undertaken at ETH, while the use of different claddings on each of the four fa- [15] cades reflect the fundamental influence of Aldo Rossi in Switzerland during this time.

But it is with the winning entry of the competition for the new Stadelhofen in Zurich that Calatrava addresses for the first time the construction of a complex space and its equally complex rapport with the context. The section organizes the space with exceptional clarity, emphasizing the deep cleft of the adjacent hill and allowing its natural rhythms to generate the overall structure of the project.

Jakem Factory, Munchwilen, Switzerland, 1983-1984

To cover this large industrial space, Calatrava designed a lightweight steel structure of open triangular-section compound girders that are stiffened by corrugated sheet metal cladding.

Each girder is made from two identical modules consisting in two steel beams, the bottom one straight and the top one curvilinear; they are joined at the bottom at right angles and connected above by the aforementioned sheet metal cladding, to which is entrusted the function of stabilizing the whole. Despite the componential character of the design, there is no clear distinction in the end between structural and cladding elements.

The single components in and of themselves offer little in the way of strength, but when linked together they create an overall structure as sturdy as it is light in weight.

The structural and engineering challenges of the project were rigorously tested and analyzed through the use of scale models.

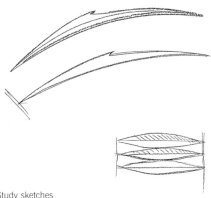

Study sketches

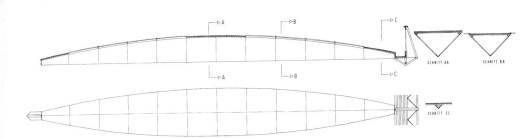

Section and plan of the roofing module

Facade

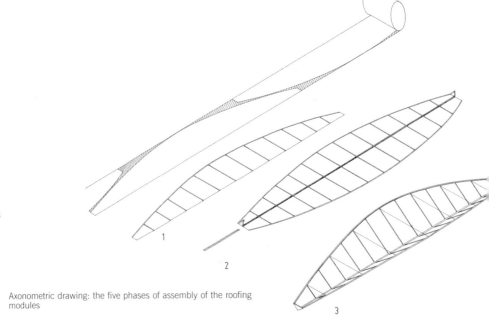

Axonometric drawing: the five phases of assembly of the roofing
modules

The roofing system

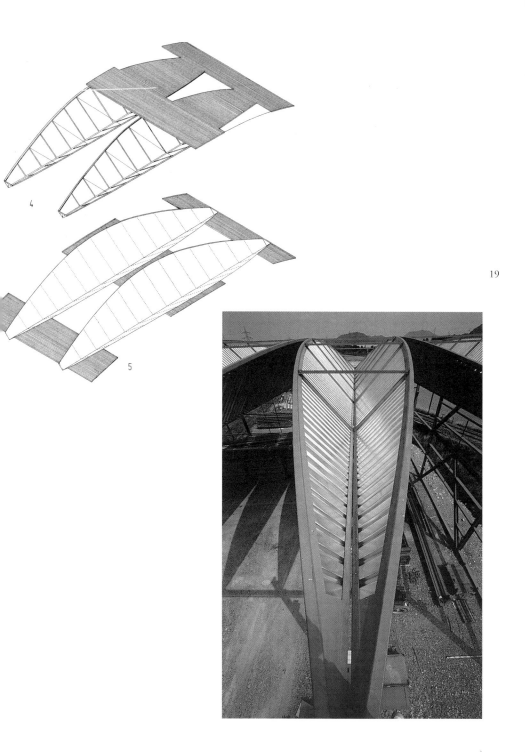

4

5

Concert Hall, Bärenmatte Community Center, Suhr, Switzerland, 1983-1988

The brief for this project was to construct a concert hall within an existing complex dedicated to community services and activities. Here, the theme of covering ample spaces with lightweight structures reaches a level of yet greater complexity; being a public performance space rather than an industrial one, the project demanded both architectural refinement and excellent acoustical qualities.

Resting upon a sequence of pilasters are the roofing modules, triangular-section box girders that meet along the central longitudinal axis of the hall. This solution perpetuates that of the Jakem factory in principle, though the girders here are not exposed but given a smooth, immaculate finish. Four chrome-plated steel cables join the lower extremities of each pair of girders, reinforcing the strength of the structure through tensile stress.

The points of contact between the framing for exterior roof cladding and the bearing structure below correspond with the central longitudinal axis and tops of the lateral facades. A band of clerestory-like windows allows natural light to suffuse the hall.

The depth and articulation of the ceiling/roof structure are also emphasized by the system of artificial illumination, which highlights both the intrados of the curved girders and the space between the load-bearing elements and the exterior cladding.

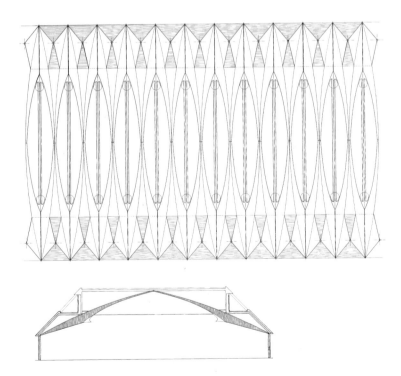

Plan of the roof and cross section of the hall

Interior of the hall

A prefabricated roofing module

Photo of the building site, demonstrating the relation of pilasters to roof

Detail of the
ceiling

Interior of the hall

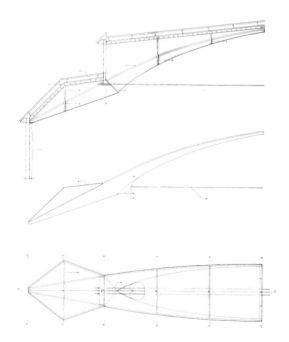

Details of the roofing modules

Fabbrica Ernstings, Coesfeld, Germania, 1983-1985

By winning a competition held by the textile manufacturer Ernstings, Santiago Calatrava, Bruno Reichlin and Fabio Reinhart thus found themselves faced with the challenge of redesigning the exterior of an existing industrial building.

The project evolves from the trio's reflections on the compositional and formal relationships among the factory's various preexisting elements. Classical principles of composition are applied to the redesign of the structure's exterior, conjugated through the use of industrial materials whose plastic qualities are accentuated.

For the cladding of the four facades of the main building, the architects modelled the base with prefabricated concrete elements, while sheet aluminum – flat, corrugated, or specially fabricated for this particular project – defines the continuity of the outer shell and carries over to the roof. Each facade is distinguished from the others by a different use of the same materials.

Calatrava's interest in what we might call "mixed", or heterogeneous construction has its roots here, and will come even more conspicuously to the fore later on. Inasmuch as preexisting structures can present irregularities that would be difficult to overcome with mere refinishing, the use of industrial materials as cladding offers advantages from both the functional and esthetic points of view, in that it allows absolute freedom at the compositional level.

The continuity of the cladding is not in any way compromised by the three principal openings, for the material and the texture of the doors are contiguous with the rest of the facade. The doors are opened by way of a singularly Calatravian system of joints that behave in a way that evokes the anatomical mechanism of the knee: when the bottom edges of the doors are raised by a motor, they fold and project outwards to create an undulating sequence of curved awnings that protect and signal the entrance.

Apart from the four facades, the project also entailed the construction of a bridge that connects the main building to a secondary structure. Both the bridge itself and the curtain wall that bounds it are entirely in steel and aluminum.

24

Views of the completed project

The doors

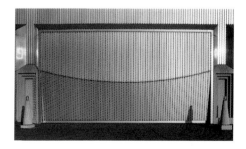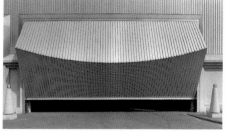

Sequence illustrating the mechanism
of the doors

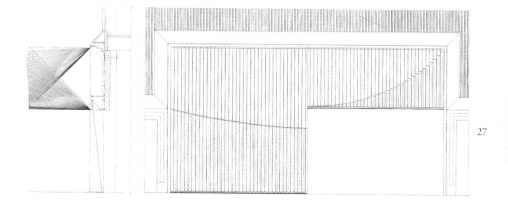

Perspective and section of a door

The cladding of one of the facades

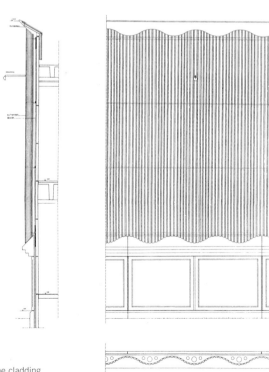

Detail of the cladding

Detail of the cladding

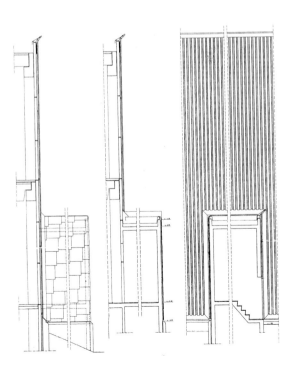

Cantonal School, Wohlen, Switzerland, 1984-1988

The project for this high school in Wohlen called for the definition, in the context of an existing building, of the four loci of greatest institutional and symbolic importance: the entrance, the atrium, the library, and the auditorium.

The form of the canopy over the entrance is generated by the intersection of two conical structures that create a long, parabolic arch.

As is often the case with Calatrava's architecture, it is the roof that assumes the strongest connotational role: the covering of the atrium is constructed with laminated V-section wooden beams disposed radially and posed atop a ring of vertical elements, supported in their turn by the bearing walls below to form a lantern. A lightweight concrete ceiling composed of four unequal, asymmetrical vaults covers the space of the library. The four vaults meet at a single point and rest there upon a single column with a marked entasis. The fact that the only other points of support are found high up on the walls creates the illusion that the entire ceiling is floating.

The canopy over the entrance is composed of a tubular steel arch from which spring the cantilevered beams that sustain a series of glass panels.

The ceiling of the *aula magna*, or auditorium, is another variation on the use of open triangular-section structural elements. Like the atrium roof, they are in laminated wood, and are held up here by inclined pilasters of reinforced concrete. Rectilinear ribs connect the dramatically arched beams to the gentle curve of the roof above.

Detail of the entrance canopy

View of the entrance

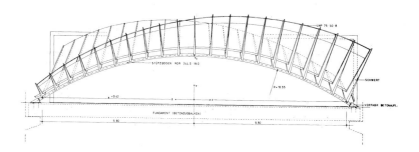

Frontal elevations

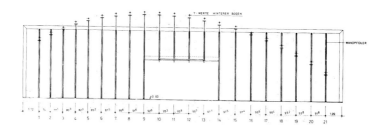

The library

The library

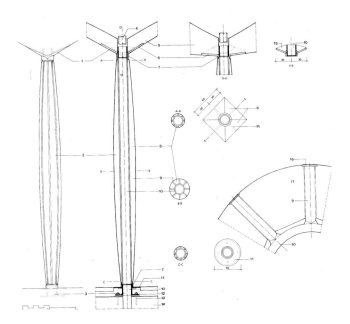

Drawing of the central
pilaster

The ceiling of the atrium

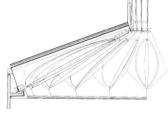

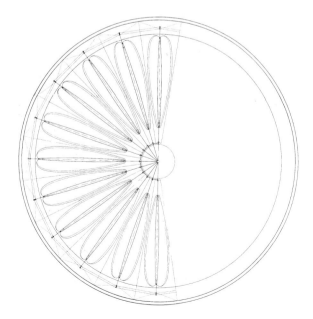

Plan and section of the atrium roof

36

The auditorium

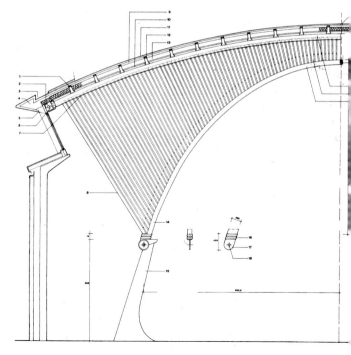

Sections

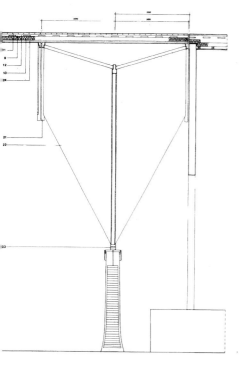

The auditorium roof under
construction

Stadelhofen Train Station,
Zurich, Switzerland, 1983-1990

"The complex systems of support and drainage, along with the tubes and cables that constitute the provisory links between the Hohe Promenade and the Stadelhofen create the impression of a highly sophisticated construction site, almost like an operating room on a geological scale: the morainic hill with its deep, open cleft between two tunnels now seems held together by cables and tensors, as if it were a wound that has been temporarily medicated. After completion of this more surgical phase comes the installation of the railway system and the superstructure of the station itself, whereby the wound of the cleft will be outfitted with a sort of refined prosthesis." (P. Nicolin, 1985)

Another winning entry, this time in a competition for the restructuring of an area situated at the foot of a hill that was once part of the city's ancient defense system, the redesign of the Stadelhofen train station is the project that brought international recognition to Santiago Calatrava and his work. Because of the importance of the Stadelhofen station in the greater metropolitan railway network, the site of the intervention occupies a central position in the urban nucleus.

A walkway covered by a pergola, the cantilevered canopy over the tracks, and an underground shopping area are the elements that constitute the architect's point of departure in reinterpreting the space of the station, a space that becomes not so much an isolated fact, an efficient means of communication with the suburbs, but rather a true public space insofar as it is capable of constructing relationships, whether operating within its own interior or on an urban scale.

The project revolves around the principle of the "cross section". The overall composition is governed by the repetition of the cross section that is maintained practically unaltered for the entire length of the intervention (270 m), finding further articulation at the point where there is an abrupt change in grade between the city and the hillside park, which is resolved through a series of bridges.

The uppermost of the structure's three levels is covered by a continuous pergola of metal arches that borders the containment wall rendered necessary by the excavation of the hillside to accomodate the third track.

The level of the tracks themselves is partially covered on the city side by a canopy of steel and glass that cantilevers out from a series of compound steel pilasters composed of one vertical and one inclined element set into a concrete base; the pilasters are connected at the top by a tubular-section girder that runs the entire length of the platform and from which the cantilevered steel ribs project.

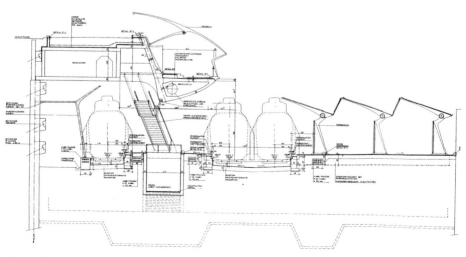

Cross sections

38

Model illustrating the relationship between the intervention and the city

The building site

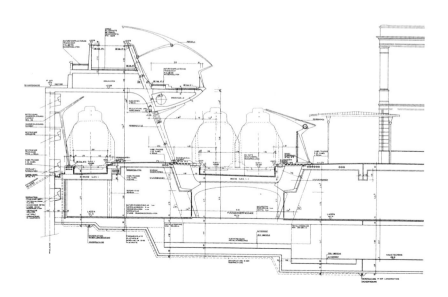

The covered passageway above the third track is supported by inclined steel pilasters outfitted with perpendicular steel plates that meet the slightly concave roof at four points.

The exploitation of the plastic qualities of reinforced concrete distinguishes the lowermost level, a subterranean passageway that hosts a number of shops. The effect of plasticity is accentuated by the natural light that filters in through the spaces between the reinforced concrete arches that constitute its structure, thanks to the use of glass brick for the platforms of the level above.

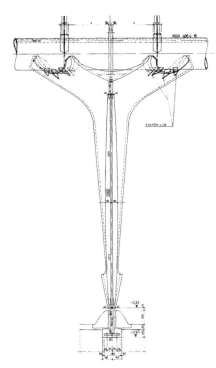

Section and elevation of the cantilevered canopy

The cantilevered canopy

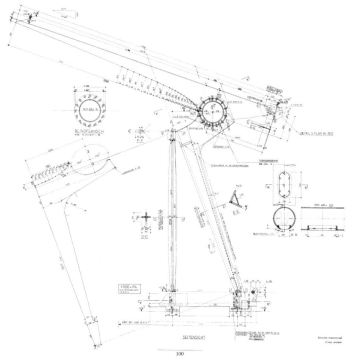

BLINDFLANSCH

DETAILS PLAN 30-2622

TORSIONSROHR

D-D

E-E

K-K   L-L

1000 × P4

SEITENLICHT

Seconde transversal
Cross section

100

The pergola

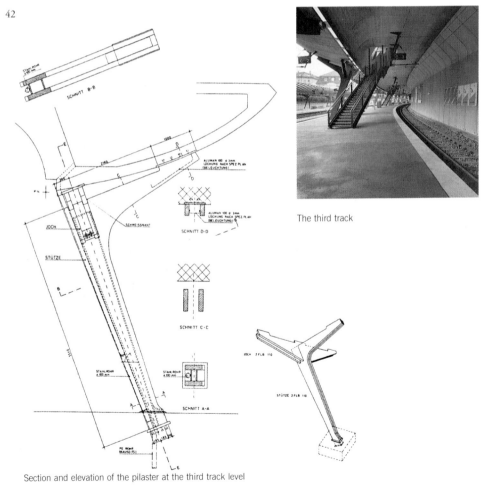

The third track

Section and elevation of the pilaster at the third track level

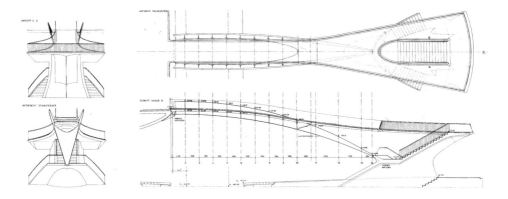

Plans and sections of the footbridge

General view

Cabaret Tabourettli, Basel, Switzerland, 1986-1987

The project for the Cabaret Tabourettli entailed the re-modelling of a medieval building, the so-called Hinter-haus, situated in the historic center of Basel. The architect's primary consideration was conditioned by the fact that the foundation of the edifice is practically non-existent, or at least unsuited to significant transformations of a structural nature.

Calatrava's plan thus had to be based on the necessary autonomy of any new bearing structures, designed in such a way as to pose no threat to the static equilibrium of the original building. One such element is a steel staircase-bridge that assumes both structural and distributive functions; the new loads comported by its introduction are concentrated in a single point on a solid and stable support.

This same non-invasive, non-destructive ethic informs the other aspects of the intervention. For the elements central to the Cabaret's function as a public locale – the bar, the coat room, the entrance spaces – Calatrava designed lightweight, movable structures which can be easily adapted to any exigency, and which above all do not compromise the existing building in any way.

The ceiling of the main hall, consisting in a series of suspended V-section wooden joists that further the research begun in the Concert Hall of the Bären-matte Community Center, is held together by a system of cables and steel braces.

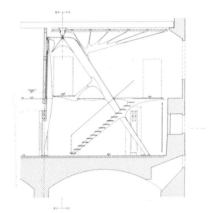

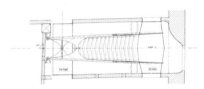

Section and plan

The staircase-bridge

The main hall

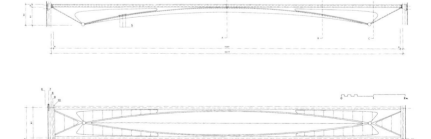

Section and plan of the ceiling

In Motion

The investigation of movement is for Calatrava a constant source of poetic and technological inspiration, insofar as it is capable of generating forms endowed with a powerful emotional and symbolic impact.

It would not be an exaggeration to call it an obsession, for movement figures into the majority of his projects, as does the evident will to provide the work of architecture and engineering with an identity potent enough to inspire amazement in even the most distracted passerby.

Subtlety and lightness of movement is coupled with an unassailable structural stability to push an already extreme limit yet further. Indeed, Calatrava's mobile works seem suspended at the edge of that limit, crystallized, stopped at just the moment before it becomes too late...

The architect's unceasing study of the growth and comportment of organic forms fuses with one of the signature char-

"Motion gives an unexpected dimension to form, making it seem a living thing.
Instead of imagining a building as something mineral, like a rock, we might begin to compare it with the sea rippling with waves, or a flower whose petals open every morning."
(Santiago Calatrava, 1997)

acteristics of the 20th century – motion – and out of this fusion emerge forms apparently without rest, forms in continuous dialogue with nature (the Kuwait Pavilion) and with the surrounding context (the Médoc river bridge, the remodelling of the Reichstag).

Sound as they are, the mechanisms that generate the movement in Calatrava's works somehow lose their substantiality, vanishing in the astonishment generated, as in the Swissbau Pavilion and the later *Shadow Machine*, where the distinction between architecture and sculpture remains highly ambiguous. In projects like the Los Angeles chapel and the more recent Milwaukee Art Museum, motion becomes selfsame as the space it creates, and form seems to condense the complex memory of the conceptual processes and the flow of information that underlie contemporary architecture.

Iba Squash Hall, Berlin, Germany, 1979

One of Calatrava's earliest projects is for the covering of two outdoor squash courts, and is part of the Kochstrasse project by Fabio Reinhart and Bruno Reichlin.

"The restless students of Aldo Rossi wanted to include an extraordinary and dynamic element in the refined historicist context of their proposal [...] In that project there was something absolutely unexpected: the pitched roof of a squash court, but movable, like the wings of a butterfly."

(P. Nicolin, 1985)

Two aerodynamic wing-section elements, constructed in wood and sheathed in copper, are supported by four tapered columns whose bases are equipped with hinges that are in turn connected to a motor.

When the motor is activated, the columns are set in motion, communicating that motion to the wings by way of a system of steel cables.

Scale model showing the wings in motion

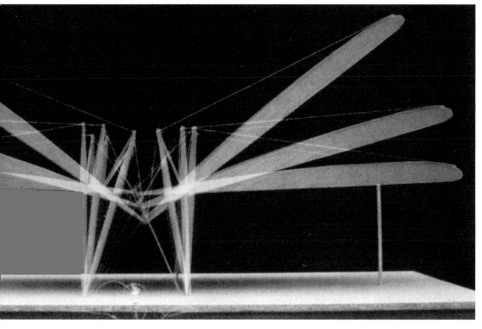

Emergency Services Center,
San Gallo, Switzerland, 1988-1998

Scale model

The theme of the project derives from a decision to concentrate all of the canton's emergency traffic control services in a single building. The choice of the site presented a certain degree of complexity, insofar as the architect had to redefine a dense area in the center of the city which, following a series of modifications effectuated at mid-century, had fallen into decline.

Specifically, the site is adjacent to the enclosure wall of the historic San Gallo monastery, in the vicinity of the centrally situated cathedral.

Calatrava proposes a basement structure, partially underground, which interprets and becomes part of the network of visual relations among the various existing buildings. The facilities housed within are illuminated from above by a large, elliptical-plan skylight, which consists in 7-cm-thick panes of reinforced glass supported by the parabolic curve of the central girder.

The problem of regulating internal temperature and light intensity in the control room is resolved by the movable *brise-soleil* that overlays the skylight, following its form. Thanks to a system of hydraulic joints, the panels affixed to the frame of the *brise-soleil* can assume a number of diverse configurations, thereby offering the possibility of many variations on the quality and intensity of light within. At night, the artificial light emanating from the glass skylight illuminates the external space.

50

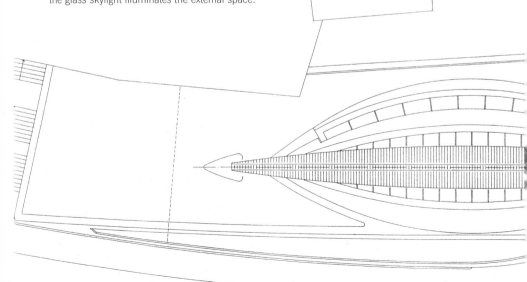

Roof plan

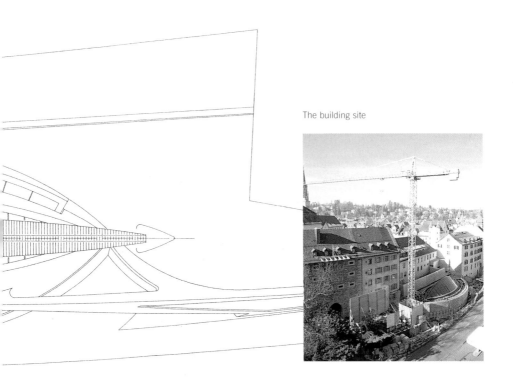

Cross section showing the movement of the *brise-soleil*

The building site

Montjuic Tower, Barcelona, Spain, 1989-1992

The celebration of the 1992 Olympic Games in Barcelona provided the opportunity to redefine numerous areas of the city, whether at the level of new sporting facilities or that of existing infrastructure and services not necessarily connected to the Games themselves, but which nonetheless reshaped the Catalan capital.

The hill of Montjuic is one such area, individuated for the construction of new spaces for sporting events and assigned a central role in the urban dynamics of the future.

The telecommunications tower that crowns Montjuic, distinguished by both its extraordinary form and high degree of visibility, lends immediate recognizability to the area.

The tower is composed of an inclined shaft with a steel superstructure resting on three points; at the top, the shaft transmogrifies into a hook that wraps around a seemingly free-floating vertical element, balancing both the weight of the structure and its composition.

The slant of the shaft coincides with that of the sun's rays on the day of the summer solstice, such that the structure functions as an enormous sundial. The tower rests upon a circular base of reinforced concrete clad in stone, inside which the telecommunications facilities are housed. Access is gained through an arched opening that frames a mechanical door which, constructed of metal slats that fold inward as the door is raised, simulates the movement of an eyelid in the process of opening.

The opening and closing of the door is regulated by an hydraulic mechanism activated by a motor.

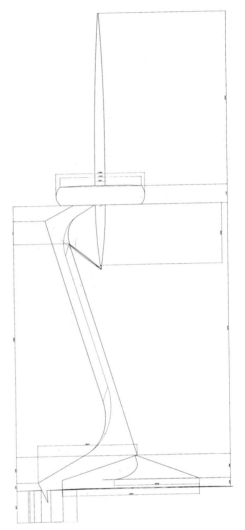

Side elevation

The building site

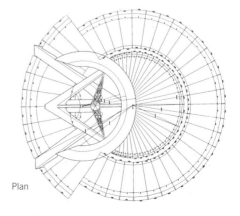

Plan

View

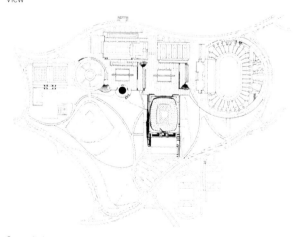

General plan

The door in closed position

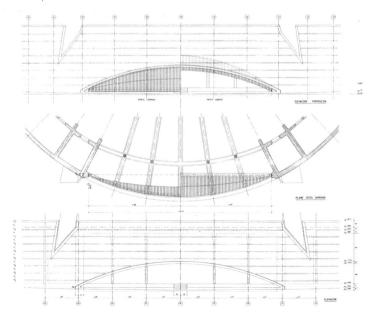

Details of the door mechanism

The door

Municipal Hall and redesign
of Plaza España, Alcoy, Spain,
1992-1995

This project is Calatrava's solution to the problem of redesigning and lending a coherent character to the central square of Alcoy, Plaza España. The architect transforms the plaza into what is effectively the roof of a *hypogeum*, a long, subterranean hall, connoted by the presence of certain monumental elements at street level that signal the entrances to the level below. These elements are characterized above all by their mobility.

At one end of the plaza is the main entrance to the municipal hall, whose mechanized opening is regulated by a motor. At the other end is a second mobile structure, this one constituted by a system of square-section steel slats of varying lengths which, when closed, lie flush with the paved surface; when its motor is activated, the slats rise and fold back, describing the movement of a wave to reveal a reflecting pool beneath.

The municipal hall, as noted, lies below street level. The containment walls follow the long and narrow triangular form of the plaza above, defining the space of the hall. The overall length is approximately 80 meters, while the width tapers from 15.6 meters at one end to 9 meters at the opposite end.

The longitudinal axis of the hall is defined by a great concrete arch, the principal bearing structure of the roof. Radiating laterally from it like the ribs of a whale are secondary arches, each symmetrical pair prefabricated and cast from the same mold. The interstices between the transverse arches are spanned by panes of reinforced glass held in place by a system of stainless steel anchors. This solution allows the *hypogeum* to be illuminated naturally, thanks to a series of narrow fissures cut into the pavement of the plaza above.

At night, when the subterranean hall is lit artificially, these same fissures create an impressive effect of blades of light issuing from the ground.

56

Scale model in motion

Drawings of the mobile structure

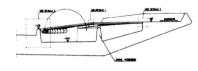

View of the plaza

Study drawing

View of the plaza

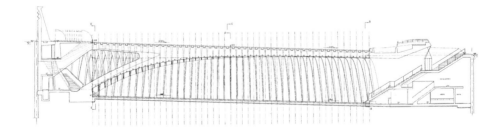

Longitudinal section

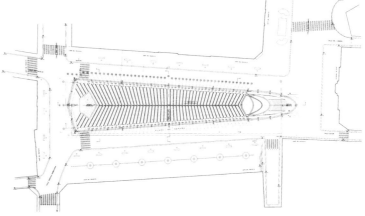

Plan of the plaza

Views of the subterranean hall

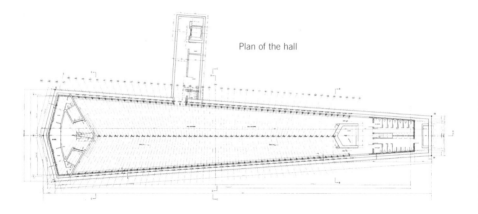

Plan of the hall

Swissbau Pavilion, Basel, Switzerland, 1989

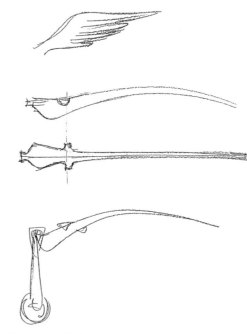

Commissioned by Switzerland's National Association of Concrete Manufacturers, the project for the pavilion was conceived as a demonstration of the extraordinary plastic possibilities of cast concrete and of prefabricated concrete elements. Calatrava addresses both questions in terms of his own interest in movable roofs and ephemeral, temporary structures.

The theme of covering and uncovering a space is integrated with that of movement, and in this case the theme of movement is inflected in such a way as to insinuate the instinct of flight, an aspiration toward lightness in a structure whose principal material paradoxically epitomizes massiveness, density, weight.

In addition to the architect's research on the functional aspects of the project, there is another type of investigation into the themes of motion and flight which is linked to images drawn from the world of natural forms, chosen in function of the possibility of transformation they represent.

Fourteen prefabricated concrete ribs are sustained by an equal number of corbels affixed to a backboard made of concrete panels. A system of drive shafts connected to synchronized rotating disks generate the undulating movement of the ribs.

Study sketches for the movable ribs

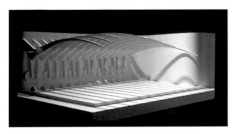

Scale model in motion

The prefabricated elements before assembly

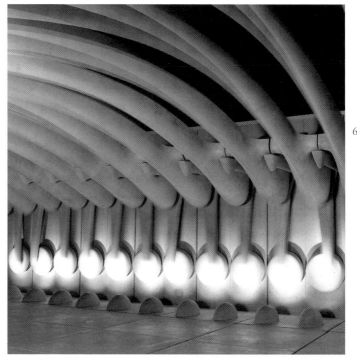

The finished work in motion

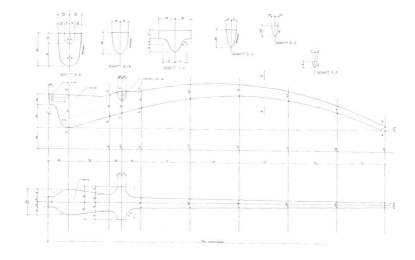

Plan, elevation
and cross sections
of one of the ribs

Shadow Machine, New York, USA, 1992-1993

The sculpture executed for the garden of New York's MoMA on the occasion of the exhibition "Structure and Expression", later to be reinstalled along the Canal Grande for the Venice Biennial, represents the architect's further investigation of the theme of motion and a further development of the research initiated at the Swissbau Pavilion in Basel.

Twelve prefabricated concrete ribs are driven by the rotary movement of the ball joints to which their extremities are attached. The independent, precisely coordinated movements of each element combine to suggest the idea of a living organism, a fluttering creature of the sea or sky.

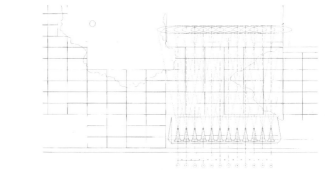

Plan

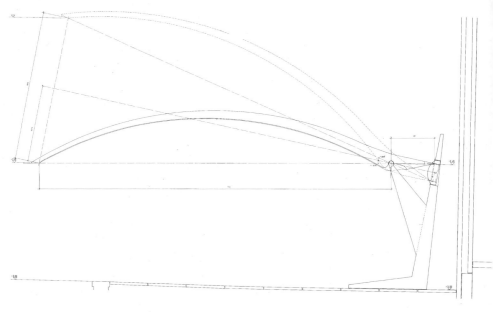

Section/elevation

The installation at MoMA

A second incarnation: overlooking Venice's Canal Grande

Floating Pavilion, Lake Lucerne, Switzerland, 1989

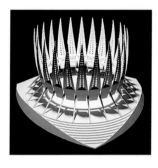

Scale model in the open position

Designed for the celebration of the 700th anniversary of the Swiss Confederation, the project is an open homage to Robert Maillart's pavilion for the Universal Exposition of 1939.

The floating structure is composed of hollow, watertight cells in reinforced concrete, was to have been anchored to the banks of Lake Vierwaldstaetter, where it would host various events programmed for the celebrations.

This artificial island, the sides of its triangular plan slightly convex, functions substantially as an auditorium with a seating capacity of 400. The auditorium is a circular structure consisting in a series of inwardly inclined pilasters which support 24 roofing modules, each in the form of a double-edged blade.

Thanks to a motor-driven system, these modules can be made to pivot on the ring that anchors them to the bearing structure. When lowered, they close to form a dome; when raised, they transform the image of the pavilion into that of a giant acquatic flower, an unmistakable point of reference with respect to its lakeside surroundings.

Scale model in the closed position

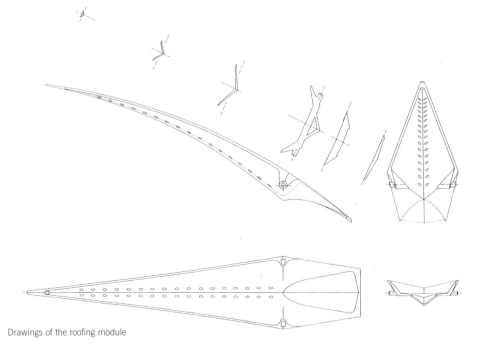

Drawings of the roofing module

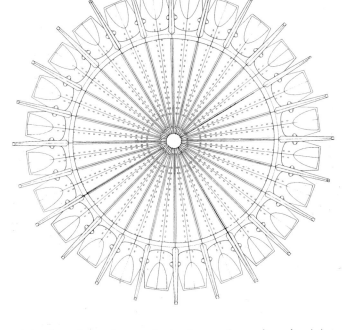

Roof plan

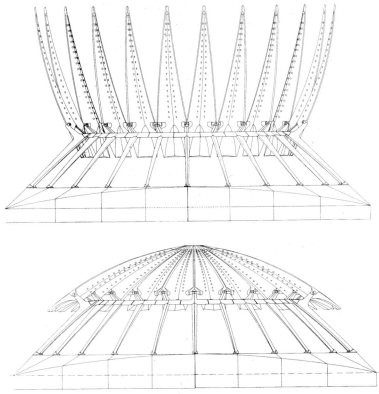

Elevations: open and closed

Kuwait Pavilion, Seville, Spain, 1991-1992

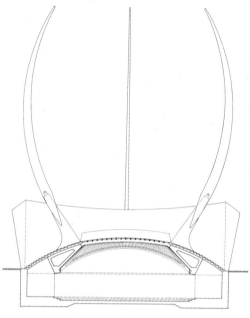

Cross section, open

The decision to include Kuwait among the countries participating in Seville's Expo '92 led to the commissioning and construction of a pavilion that would reaffirm, once the Gulf War was over, Kuwait's role in the international community.

The symbolic charge that emanates from this temporary structure is connoted by the powerful expressivity of a formal choice that privileges and instills a sense of wonder. From the outside the pavilion reads as a sort of raised platform set upon a stepped base and closed on two sides by curved concrete walls. Two staircase-ramps conduct one to an ample hall at the underground level designed to host an exhibition.

The project's cross section is distinguished by the contiguity of the surface of the raised platform and the access stairways on either side, which combine to create a graceful, uninterrupted curve, like a segment of a cylindrical section. This structure is supported by compound wooden girders of open triangular section which are visible from the exhibition space on the lower level.

Set upon longitudinal beams in hollow concrete, these girders cover a span of 14 meters. Their arched form is accentuated by the rhythmic repetition of wooden elements that run from their dramatically curved underside to the softer bow of the ceiling above. The spaces between these elements allow natural light to filter into the exhibition hall through the flooring of the upper level, which is made with slabs of translucent marble bonded to stratified glass and supported by a slightly convex rectilinear grid.

As for the floor of the exhibition hall, its configuration follows that of the ceiling: the central area directly beneath the arched wooden girders is paved in black marble with white insets, while the raised perimeter, delineated by the longitudinal support beams, is entirely in white marble.

The roof over the upper level is composed of 17 wooden elements, each 25 meters long, whose form recalls that of a palm frond. They are supported by leaning pilasters in reinforced concrete which also serve to define the threshold between inside and out.

A hydraulic system of counterweights allows the rib-like roof elements to rotate on the tube girder that joins them to the pilasters; since each rib moves independently, the possibilities of the different configurations that the structure can assume are effectively unlimited.

By day, the platform assumes a protected, shaded attitude, while at night it transforms into a totally open space for the projection of slides and videos.

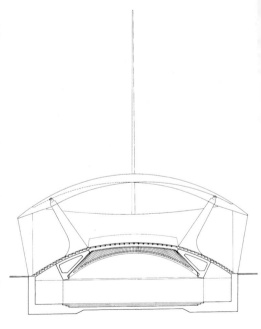

Cross section, closed

The exhibition hall

The platform

Fabricating the wooden girders for the ceiling of the exhibition hall

View of the pavilion

Chapel of the Tomb of Brother Junipero
Los Angeles, USA, 1996

Responding to an invitational competition for the construction of the new Catholic cathedral in Los Angeles, Calatrava offers a highly personal interpretation of what is meant by sacred space.

As in his other works, the simultaneous presence of multiple themes, both technical and poetic, also characterizes this one. The space of prayer and meditation enclosed by the excavated base of the structure recalls the hermit's grotto and communicates a sense of profound spirituality, free of obvious external signs.

In its relation to the outside, the mobile element that perches atop the monument strives to define the contours of a visual and emotional event that captures the imagination while at the same time acting as both landmark and signal to the city.

Another distinctive feature of the project is the mirroring of the chapel in a reflecting pool, exquisitely appropriate metaphor of the transition from the material to the spiritual. Linear elements radiating out from an inclined armature describe a movement in space that might suggest the flight of a swan. The degree of aperture of this species of mono-wing determines the intensity of the light that enters the chapel below.

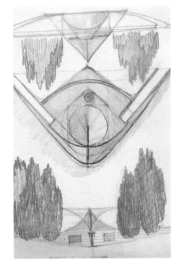

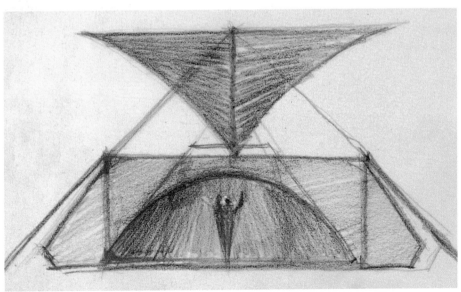

Sketches

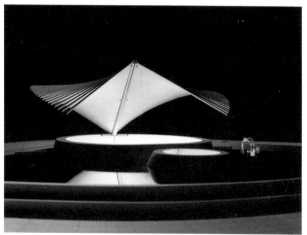

Scale model in motion

Cover, Consolidate, Connect

The covering of broad spans, the overhead protection of large public spaces has always been one of the driving forces behind the making of architecture.

It is in the design of truly large buildings that the architect often concentrates much of his or her formal and technical experimentation.

The coverings of such spaces are laboratories wherein one can push limits to their extremes and challenge the boundaries of existing technology, where the roof becomes at once symbol and subtle membrane between earth and sky, a striving toward the light, a progressive dissolution of apparent structure.

This path, whose course has been marked out over the past two centuries by the works of great engineer-architects, is the path chosen by Santiago Calatrava, in whose work the challenge of covering ever larger and more complex spaces, in our day rendered possible by the almost unlimited options offered through new materials and technology, feeds his conviction that a building lend a powerful identity to its site, powerful enough to override technical expedients through the elabora-

"The hand / the hand takes measure / the hand touches / evaluates, examines, appreciates / ... it opens and closes / two hands joined / union of unions / two hands joined / to protect, to receive, or to reject / they cover, they hide, they conceal / they reveal / they bid hello or goodbye / they dance together with the arms / simulating the waves of the sea"
(Santiago Calatrava, 1995)

tion of a figurative language that places the symbolic and evocative value of architectural form at the forefront.

From the four "microhistories" with which Calatrava narrated the spaces of the Wohlen high school to his design for Toronto's BCE Gallery, one can see how natural forms and figurative concerns take precedence over purely technical ones – or better, how they absorb and exploit them.

In the BCE project, the notion of support is metaphorized in the form of a tree in a composition that plays illusionistically with light and shadow so as to veil the mystery of its own structural identity; a game that will later turn up in the projects for Spitalfields Gallery in London, for the Train Stations 77 of Spandau, Lieges and Lisbon, and for the restoration of Berlin's Reichstag.

In this latter, extremely complex work, the redefinition of the identity of the former chancelry is effectuated through a refined reelaboration of the existing glass roofs, such that the entire building seems to converge toward the new cupola, which stands as a symbol of rebirth, of transformation, and above all of vision.

Canopy for a Bus and Tram Stop,
Zurich, Switzerland, 1989

Following the curvature of the tram tracks, the
canopy is composed of a central longitudinal beam
sustained by inclined pilasters whose bases incorporate benches for waiting passengers.

Cantilevering out from the beam are the
steel wings that support a peripheral frame and the
panes of glass that constitute the roof, which becomes opaque at its extremities.

The slant of the two end pilasters follows
the longitudinal axis, while that of the two central
ones – different in both form and profile from the
outer pair – runs perpendicular to it.

These central pilasters are glassed in on
three sides, providing additional shelter against
wind and foul weather.

Scale model

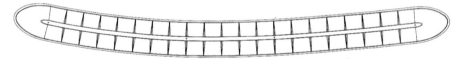

Plans, sections

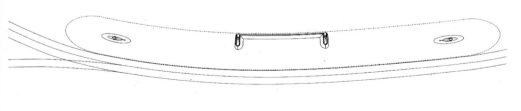

Canopy for a Bus Stop,
San Gallo, Switzerland, 1989-1996

The project for the San Gallo bus stop canopy revolves around themes both formal and structural in
nature, while at the same time reflecting carefully
upon the characteristics specific to the urban context in which it is destined to find itself.

The dimensions of the structure are somewhat unusual for Calatrava, insofar as it is not
meant to be perceived on a large urban scale. As
such, it posits itself as a new and autonomous element in an existing context that is in itself fragmen-
tary and disarticulate, yet it somehow suggests a
possible order by defining a sort of spatial threshold
capable of independently sparking new relationships between the elements that make up the surrounding urban context.

A circular-section beam provides anchorage
for a sequence of curved steel blades which in turn
support a roof of reinforced glass; this beam rests
upon two inclined pilasters to which are affixed a
pair of retractable steel and glass wings which can
be opened to provide additional shelter.

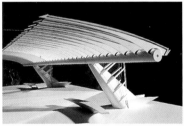

79

Scale model

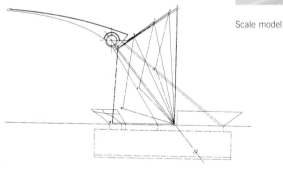

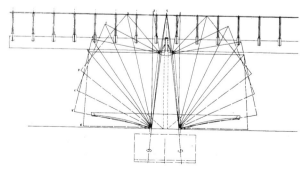

Elevations

Modular Subway Station,
London, Great Britain, 1992

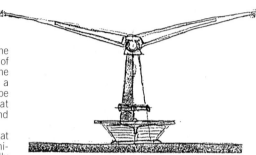

Study sketch

This project is part of a program sponsored by the London public transit authority for the renovation of the city's subway system, which dates back to the 1930s. Calatrava's task was to come up with a modular design for a subway station that could be applied throughout the entire system and that would unify said system on both the visual and functional levels.

Working from the premise of a canopy that incorporates an enclosed waiting room, the architect devised a system of base elements specifically tailored to the transit authority's stated needs.

A circular-section torsion beam with a cantilevered canopy is the basic module: for the central platforms, the canopy is flat and projects from both sides of the central beam; for the lateral platforms, it is slightly curved and projects from only one side.

The vertical supports are composed of two inclined elements to which the longitudinal beam is attached. The waiting rooms beneath the canopy are enclosed by an opaque shell of sheet metal interrupted by gullwing-type glass windows that can be opened and closed.

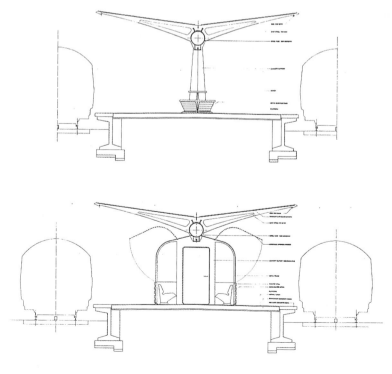

Cross sections

Scale model. Central
platform module

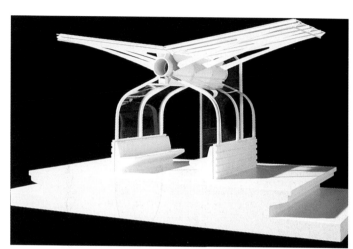

81

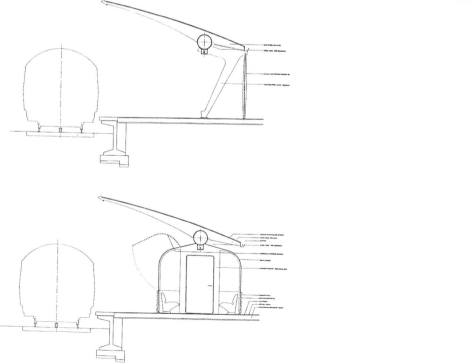

Station Hall, Lucerne, Switzerland, 1983-1989

The brief for the renovation of Lucerne's railway station called for the realization of a new lobby which, on the basis of the changing conditions of passenger, freight and vehicular traffic, would resolve the problems of distribution and of access from the plaza in front of the station and the parking garage beneath it. Calatrava's solution was to attach a new structure to the facade of the existing one, denoting it as a transitional zone, an overtly public space that explicitly avoids the conventional notion of continuity between the interior of a building and the city outside. At the same time, the new "colonnade" – an appropriate term for the classical values it embodies – announces itself as an important urban presence by dominating and defining its own side of the plaza.

The interior of the expansive glass-walled atrium, 14 meters high and 109 meters long, is articulated on three levels: a basement floor dedicated to retail trade, the ground floor to passenger services, and an upper floor that hosts a restaurant.

The structure of the atrium consists in a series of 16 prefabricated concrete pilasters of variable section and complex profile. These are stabilized by tapered steel columns that measure out the spaces between them and support the lightweight steel and glass roof that seems suspended over the vast entrance area.

From the tops of these 16 pilasters run an equal number of cables that penetrate the glass roof to anchor themselves to the steel girders that sustain its weight. The ends of the elongated "X" form assumed by these girders meet in correspondence with the concrete pilasters, creating at the structural level the grid to which the external cables are anchored while at the same time emphasizing at the formal level the main lines of stress.

Side view

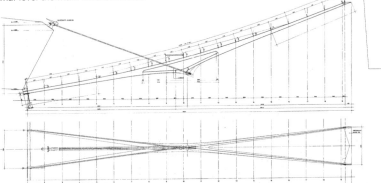

Plan and section showing the suspension system of the roof

The *hall*

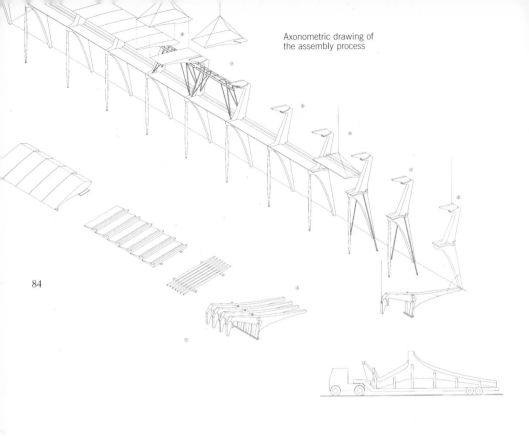

Axonometric drawing of
the assembly process

Detail of the cornice

The "colonnade"

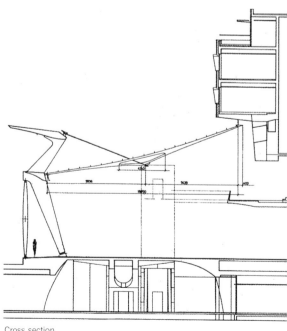

Cross section

Bauschänzli Restaurant, Zurich, Switzerland, 1988

For this open-air restaurant on a fortified island on Lake Zurich, Calatrava experiments with a roofing solution that he will repeat in a number of subsequent projects (BCE Place Gallery, Spandau Station, et. al.).

Nine "arboriform" steel supports branch out like slender trees as they rise to receive a lightweight canopy composed of movable elements.

In the closed position, the terrace is completely covered; in the open position, the corners of each module fold back to reveal alternating squares of sky.

The service facilities of the restaurant are housed in a subterranean level beneath the terrace.

Scale model of the canopy: open and closed

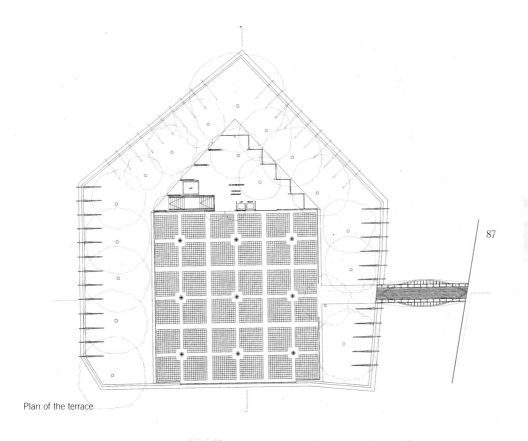

Plan of the terrace

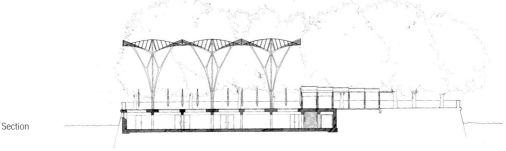

Section

Muri Monastery, Canton d'Argovia, Switzerland, 1989

The architect's task here was to design a ceiling for a large space within one of the most important Benedictine monasteries in Switzerland.

The chief concern of the project was to ensure that the intervention would not in any way disturb the structural integrity of the existing medieval structure.

Calatrava responded to that concern by designing a lightweight wooden covering that is completely autonomous with respect to the original walls of the space it covers, set as it is upon 14 freestanding columns.

Innumerable straight planks are assembled to create a single, undulating form whose upper profile is a gentle parabola while the lower part describes a tighter curve.

The intrinsic lightness of the ceiling is further accentuated by the play of light and shadow.

Three views of the scale model

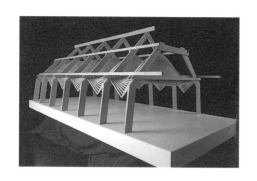

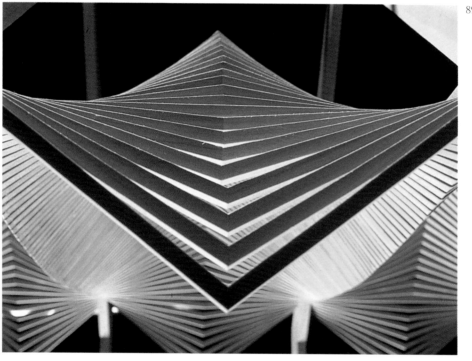

PCW Housing Complex, Würenlingen, Switzerland, 1987-1996

Commissioned by a real estate developer, this project for the low-density urbanization of an area just outside the city of Zurich is distinguished by the extensive use of reinforced concrete and prefabricated concrete elements, and by the dramatic reduction of the structures' contact with the ground.

The complex comprises 24 free-standing single-family houses disposed in two rows and three clusters of contiguous residences of six units each. The development is situated opposite a mountainous escarpment on a gently sloped plot of land.

The two rows of single-family houses, disposed back to back, are characterized by an extreme proximity between one unit and another. And yet they are sufficiently isolated so that light penetrates the spaces between them, illuminating their interiors as well as accentuating the sculptural qualities of the concrete.

The main entrance, dining area and kitchen are located on the ground floor, while directly above is the living area, which offers a view of the forest and access to the garden. The sleeping area, on the uppermost level, cantilevers out over the entrance and is partially lit by a skylight. Each unit has an underground basement.

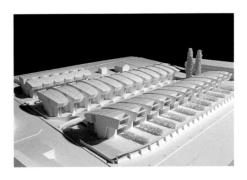

Scale model of the complex

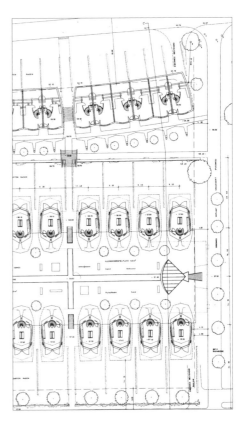

Plan

One of the groups of contiguous units

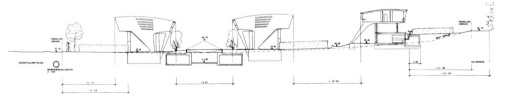

Cross section

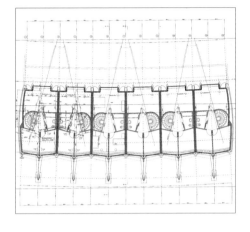

Free-standing unit: second floor plan

92

Scale model of a free-standing unit

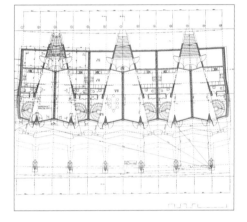

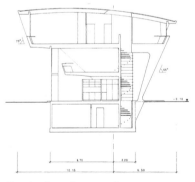

Free-standing unit: cross section

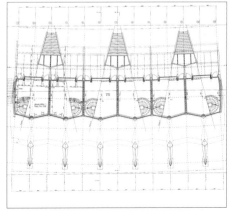

Contiguous unit: ground floor, second floor and third floor plans

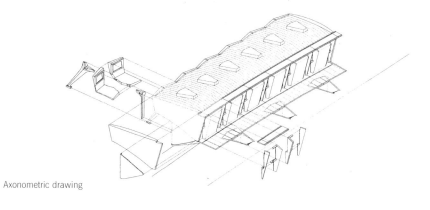

Axonometric drawing

A group of contiguous units

BCE Place Gallery, Toronto, Canada, 1987-1992

Having won the architectural competition held in 1987 for the redesign of the unused areas of Toronto's Bay Street Place, an irregularly shaped block historically acknowledged as the cultural heart of the city, Calatrava proposed a plan to cover two large public spaces, with the aim of lending structure and order to the otherwise disjointed relationships between the existing buildings.

In keeping with the North American tradition of vast covered spaces, Calatrava designed a gallery and plaza, conceiving them as independent architectural episodes yet articulating them through the same formal and technical language.

The gallery – 130 meters long, 14 meters wide, and some five stories high – is assigned the function of establishing coherent relationships between the various activities conducted in the buildings that flank it, the subterranean network of pedestrian passageways, and the space of the city itself. Inclined steel pilasters bifurcate at mid-height, the fork again higher up, such that each one sustains four of the parabolic arches of the ceiling. Longitudinal elements define the arches volumetrically, creating the effect of a barrel vault. The narrow interstices between these elements allowing natural light entering through the glazed roof above to penetrate the interior of the gallery.

The entrance to this monumental space is signalled by an awning, which is essentially a continuation of the structure that projects out past the facades of the buildings on either side of it.

Heritage Square, a space measuring about 30 meters per side, inspired Calatrava to employ a modular system of "arboriform" steel pilasters that obey the same logic of double bifurcation as those used in the gallery.

The space is covered by nine square roof modules (see the Bauschänzli restaurant project, Zurich), each crossed diagonally by two arches which are supported, as the case may be, by the pilasters or the brick facades of the buildings on its perimeter.

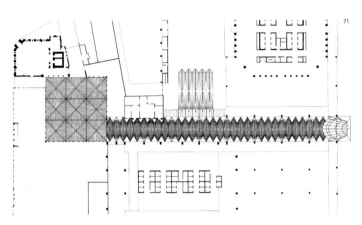

Plan of the roofs

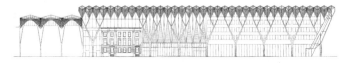

Longitudinal section

The Gallery

The Gallery: detail of the roof

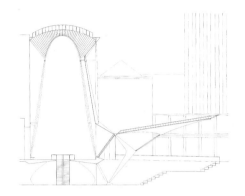

Cross section of the Garden Court
entrance

The entrance awning

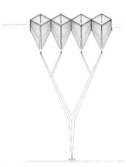

The gallery

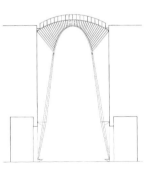

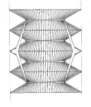

Cross section of the gallery,
elevation, plan of the roof

Spitalfields Gallery, London, Great Britain, 1990

As in the case of Toronto's Bay Street project, Calatrava was faced here with the dual task of covering a large gallery and a public square.

And again, as in Toronto, he resorted to the theme of the tree in designing the pilasters for the gallery, this time emphasizing even further the vertiginous height of the glass-roofed structure.

The plaza is delimited by a circular-plan structure composed of inclined pilasters that support ribbed roof elements which together form a low dome.

Attached at their extremities to the pilasters and the central point of the structure by swivel joints, a motorized mechanism causes these elements to rotate 90° on their longitudinal axis, thereby opening the dome and uncovering the space.

Scale model of the gallery

Scale model of the dome: closed and open

Scale model of the gallery

Cathedral of St. John the Divine,
New York, USA, 1991

This is Calatrava's winning entry in the invitational competition for the completion of the neo-Gothic cathedral situated on Manhattan's upper west side, construction of which was begun in 1892.

The competition announcement required that the participants reflect on the existing structural system and to then submit designs for the parts of the edifice that remain incomplete, meaning the entire south transept, part of the north transept, and the tops of the towers.

Also included among the requisites was a project for a biological refuge.

The solution proposed by Calatrava insists, from both a conceptual and formal point of view, on the theme of the tree, thus harking back to the archetypal forces that animated the construction of the great Gothic cathedrals.

In a process of poetic association that assimilates the crypt with roots, the nave with earth, and so forth, the architect imagined a structure sheathed in granite and limestone that branches out like a forest, extending into the existing parts of the cathedral's interior.

In Calatrava's plan, a slender, ephemeral spire soars over the crossing of the nave and transept, and the entire roof becomes a vast greenhouse whose summit is fully 55 meters above ground level.

Plan of the greenhouse

Scale model

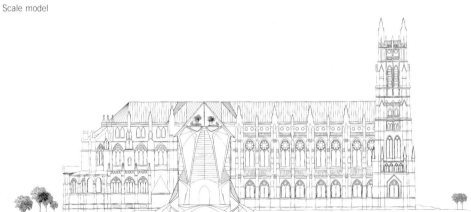

Cross section of the transept

102

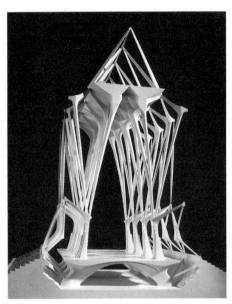

Scale model of the structural system

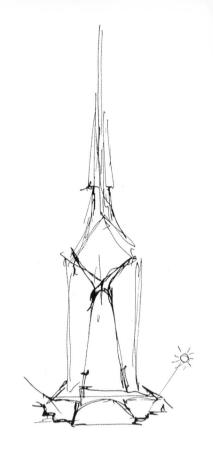

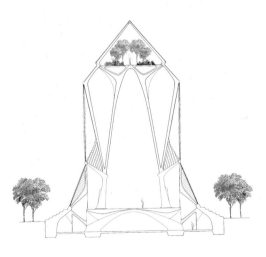

Cross section of the south transept

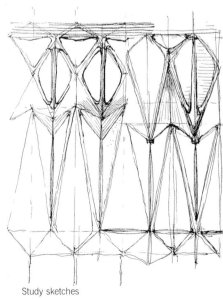

Study sketches

Scale model

Renovation and expansion of the
Reichstag, Berlin, Germany, 1992

The transfer of Parliament of the then newly unified Germany from Bonn to Berlin is the motive behind the international invitational competition announced in 1992 for the renovation and expansion of the Reichstag, traditional seat of the national legislature up until the Second World War.

Calatrava adopts an attitude of respect for the existing building, designed in 1883 by Paul Wallot, and for the site on which it stands. The objective is to redefine the Reichstag's meaning, from both the architectural and historical points of view.

Though it introduces significant new architectural elements, the plan does not seek so much to create a counterpoint between the old and the new as to recover the original image of the Reichstag through the addition of a cupola that reproduces the profile and dimensions of the destroyed original. While the intention to preserve Wallot's system of proportions is evident, Calatrava reflects carefully on the meaning that such an intervention might have in contemporary times, and seeks to go beyond mere philologically correct reconstruction so as to establish a dialectical relationship between recuperation and reinvention. Through the employment of modern building technologies, the architect has designed an extremely lightweight, transparent structure that allows for the natural illumination of the assembly hall, thus not only reinterpreting the cupola as the potent urban symbol of Wallot's original conception, but recasting the relationship between interior and exterior, metaphor of that between the legislative activities conducted within and their consequences in the world without.

The original Reichstag

Model: distribution of stress in the cupola

Study sketch

Scale model

Calatrava does not hesitate to embrace and elaborate upon certain of Wallot's other solutions, such as the glass-brick flooring of the library.

The need to provide new office and service space for the parliamentarians resulted in the extension of the building toward the east; an underground corridor connects the main structure to a new one that incorporates an ample glass-walled gallery and the various party headquarters.

The plenary assembly hall is situated on the ground floor directly beneath the cupola. The glazed ceiling, which provides the hall with natural illumination, can be opened to allow the public to observe the parliamentary proceedings.

The cupola itself is like a diaphonous membrane, a fine grid of steel whose structural integrity is sustained by a system of cables.

The four courts adjacent to the hall are also roofed in glass, such that natural light penetrates even the deepest recesses of the building.

The project that Calatrava submitted to the competition did not make the final selection, but the winning entry employs certain of its solutions.

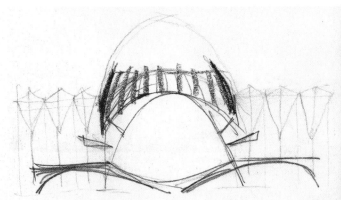

Photomontage

New Territorial Signs

The theme of 'roofing' the city is progressively amplified to the territorial scale; the vault, the shell, the cupola are among the regulative elements of a new extra-urban architecture, obligatory reference points in a wider landscape.

Projects such as the Lyon-Satolas TGV station, the concert hall in Tenerife and the Milwaukee Art Musuem pose the problem of establishing a formal and symbolic identity for contemporary architecture in the context of a decentralized territory devoid of recognizable heirarchies.

The powerful plastic and expressive force of these enormous 'machines' is often the fruit of an overlapping of the architect's relentless formal research and a specific request on the

"Calatrava seems to place in question the very notion of the building. Indeed, what is there of the traditional concept of a railway station at Stadelhofen? [...] How do we define the edifice at Alcoy? Perhaps we might call them pavilions, artificial terrains, canopies, but surely not stations, restaurants, museums or planetariums: their intended function does not effect their formal configuration at all. Perhaps we should think of them less as buildings and more as fragments of a new landscape [...]"
(Mirko Zardini, 1995)

part of the patron that the resulting structure assume a powerful physical presence with respect to its environs (thus the
spectacular entrance hall of the Lyon-Satolas station, or the
great 'horn' of the Tenerife concert hall).
Calatrava's formal and spatial research also generates elements that become typological matrices for more complex
compositions. The geometries applied at Lyon and Tenerife
multiply and evolve in the projects for the Sondico-Bilbao
and Barajas-Madrid airports; the roof motif at Montreal is
further developed in the projects for the Spandau-Berlin and
Lieges railway stations, and becomes the distinguishing feature of Lisbon's Oriente Station.

Sondica Airport, Bilbao, Spain, 1990

The project for Sondica airport was commissioned by the city of Bilbao in response to the rapidly developing metropolis' need for more extensive air transport facilities. The new airport is essentially an addition to the existing one, and is designed so as to allow for the possibility of even further expansion in the future.

The central idea of the project is that of an ample yet compact terminal delimited by vast glass surfaces.

Articulated on four levels, it is noteworthy for the simplicity of the overall plan, the efficiency with which internal traffic is organized, and the ease with which passengers can orient themselves – these qualities being due to the fact that the entirety of the space is comprehensible from any point within it.

From the central nucleus of the passenger terminal, the rest of the project develops without impediment. Two lateral wings host the arrival and departure gates and all the administrative offices; plans for a four-story parking garage linked to the terminal are currently underway.

The structure is constituted by a system of pilasters, girders and arches in reinforced concrete that combine to support a ribbed metal roof, more or less triangular in plan and characterized by a complex volumetric articulation. The wings are covered instead by a double vaulted roof of steel ribs and braces mounted on concrete pilasters.

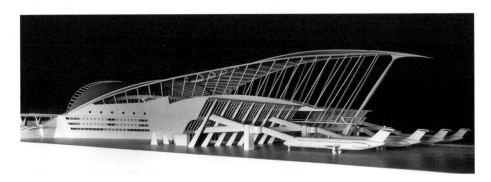

Scale model

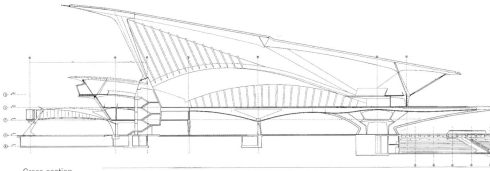

Cross section

Elevations of the north and south facades

Scale model

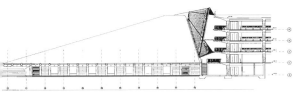

Barajas Airport, Madrid, Spain, 1997

This project is Calatrava's response to a competition announced by the Madrid air transport authorities for the design of a new terminal to supplement Barajas Airport's existing one.

The objective of the competition was to consolidate the city's airport infrastructure and to increase its capacity to accomodate air traffic between Spain and Latin America.

As in Bilbao, Calatrava's design is conceived in a modular way so as to allow for the eventual construction of additional structures in the shortest possible time period.

The core of the plan is the triangular structure that hosts the main hall of the passenger terminal, the central vertebra of a sort of spinal column made up of a sequence of smaller modules, each with a similarly triangular vaulted roof.

The planning of the interior spaces is aimed at minimizing the distances that passengers must travel by foot while maximizing the rapidity and flexibility of connections. The interaction between pedestrian and vehicular traffic is effectuated through efficient 'interfaces' positioned along the facade.

The various functions of the facility are organized so as to reduce interference between incompatible activities. The complex is essentially articulated on three levels: arrivals, departures, and internal services.

As for the airport's physical presence in relation to its surroundings and the image it seeks to project, Calatrava's project foresees the integration of the structure into a new park that will be created in front of the terminal.

112

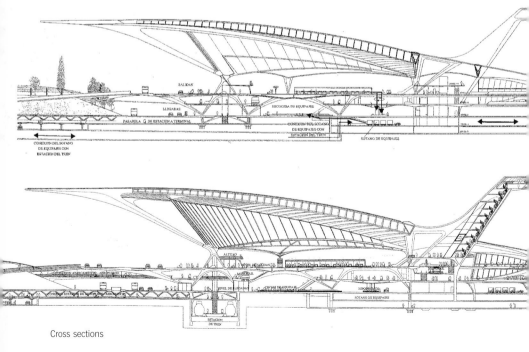

Cross sections

Scale model

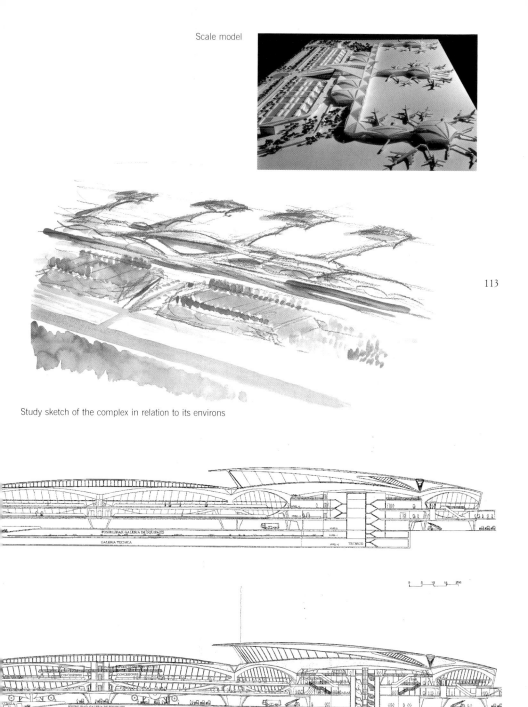

Study sketch of the complex in relation to its environs

Rhône-Alpes TGV Station, Satolas, Lyon, France, 1989-1994

The project for this high-speed railway station, built to serve Satolas Airport, is defined through elements that create relationships of scale with the existing airport structures and maintain a continuous rapport with them in terms of both visibility and functional integration.

The project presents itself as an autonomous object, capable not only of proclaiming its formal incisiveness on a territorial scale, but also of functioning efficiently and meeting the needs of a major international hub of interconnected air and rail transport.

The station's design is organized around two elements: the train tunnel and the great central hall. This latter acts as a formal and functional fulcrum between its surroundings and the track area, satisfying the fundamental condition of efficiency with regard both the accomodation of passengers and the facilitation of connections between airport and rail station. The high visibility and above all legibility of the structure allows passengers to orient themselves easily despite the complexity of its system of internal relations and multiplicity of levels.

The structure of the hall is generated by the intersection of two conical sections and is supported by reticulated arches springing from reinforced concrete supports that cover a span of approximately 100 meters. These arches define the profile of the north and south facades, both of which are entirely glazed.

The roof of the track area is characterized by a structure of concrete ribs supported by Y-shaped pilasters. The openings between the ribs illuminate the gallery with natural light.

Sculpture

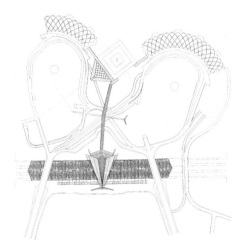

Overall plan

Views of the hall and the train gallery

The hall

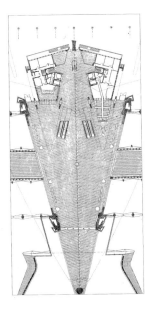

Plan of the hall

Detail showing the concrete supports and the roof of the hall

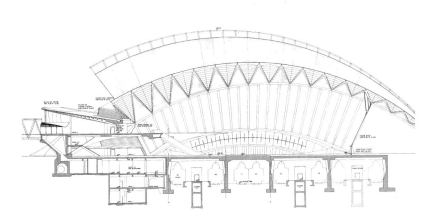

Longitudinal section

Cross section of the train gallery

The suspended walkway

The train gallery

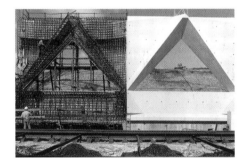

The building site

The train gallery

Jahn Sportpark, Berlin, Germany, 1992

The sporting facilities of the Jahn Sportpark were the object of a competition held by the German authorities as part of Berlin's campaign to host the 2000 Olympics. The competition called for the design of a boxing stadium, the creation of a park of at least 10 hectares to occupy the strip of land that once hosted the Wall, a study for a residential complex along the western border of the Mauerpark, the redesign of the Falkplatz, a project for a city gate, and the redefinition of the intersection of the Schoenhauserallee and Cantianstrasse.

Calatrava's proposal develops from the idea of reconstituting the original urban structure by way of an ample park which both contains all of the sporting facilities requested and at the same time provides the necessary tools for overcoming the existing divisions and integrating the various, heretofore separate urban areas surrounding it.

The most interesting architectural solutions are concentrated in the boxing stadium: a lightweight reinforced concrete superstructure in the form of a suspension bridge seems to soar over a roof that in turn appears to float above the stadium, the foundation of which integrates effortlessly into the gently undulating terrain of the park.

The roof consists in a longitudinally oriented system of arches to which perpendicular steel joists are fixed.

The central span of the main arch is constituted by a steel box girder that offers additional support to the roof below. The entrances and exits are situated beneath the transverse stabilizing arches at each end of the main arch.

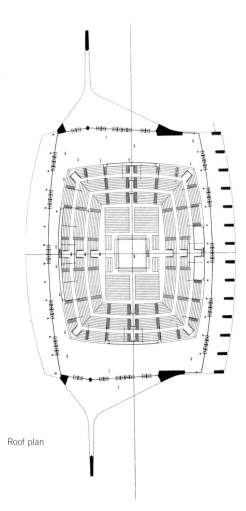

Roof plan

Elevation

Scale model of the sporting facilities

Spandau Train Station,
Berlin, Germany, 1991

The concept underlying the project for the Spandau station, developed in response to an invitational competition, operates on two different scales. On the one hand, the architect considers the relationships the project might establish between the various parts of its immediate urban surroundings – that is, between the historic city center, Wilhelmstadt and the area along the banks of the river Havel; on the other, he considers factors that express themselves on the broader metropolitan scale. In light of the changes in the very nature of the territory surrounding Berlin that followed on the heels of German reunification, and thanks to the high level of accessibility that Spandau presently enjoys (it is served by subway, suburban and interurban rail lines), a new role for the city is foreseen within Berlin's greater metropolitan area.

The project for the station evolves from the need to create a public space that satisfies the exigencies of a heavily trafficked intersection of different means of transportation while at the same time asserting itself as a significant urban presence, capable of influencing the architectural character of the city. The achievement of these objectives is sought in the negation of the idea of the railway-as-barrier, of the notion of the train station as an irregularity in the urban fabric.

Calatrava, playing on the distinctively Berlinese iconography of the elevated railway, designed an elevated platform upon which the tracks run. The platform, aside from ensuring free circulation in the north-south direction, covers a public space that functions as a connective element between two wooded parks; the pilasters supporting the roof over the platform engage the metaphor of the tree as an element of connection between architecture and nature. The platform is bounded perpendicularly on either side by two tall office buildings, each cut down the middle by ample, glassed-in galleries that run their entire height.

Another group of buildings defines the southern boundary of the park.

Study sketch

Sections

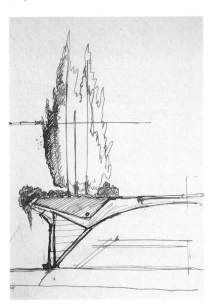

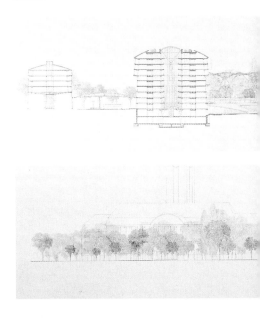

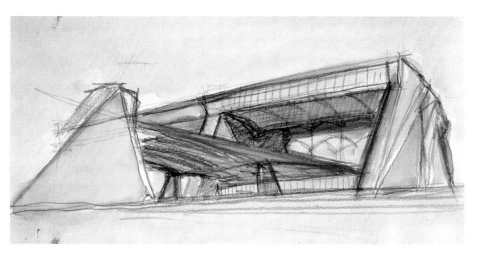

Study sketch

Scale model

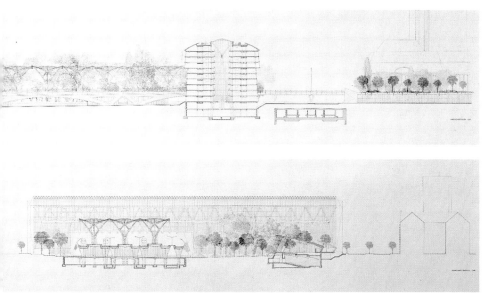

TGV Station, Lieges,
Belgium, 1996

The new complex is composed of various interconnected elements, foremost among which are the great central hall that distributes passengers to the service areas, and the structures at the eastern and western extremities that host those services less strictly linked to the transportational concerns of the station proper.

Situated at the rear of the complex and below the level of the tracks are the administrative offices, station services and the physical plant. At this same level, a connecting passageway aligned with the axis of the central hall provides access to the five train platforms.

The architectural treatment of this passageway is conceived so as to facilitate passenger orientation. The structural elements in exposed white concrete are emphasized; it is illuminated by natural light from above as well as by indirect artificial light that emanates from hidden sources.

The passenger terminal is approximately 200 meters long, its central tract symmetrical with respect to the north-south axis. The lightweight, arched roof that distinguishes it extends asymmetrically toward the east to cover the tracks.

The definitive site of the station has been pushed back somewhat with respect to the original plan in order that the complex be integrated in the most harmonious and efficient possible way into the urban fabric.

A shopping plaza occupies an area along the western side of the first track.

In certain parts of the complex the floors are made of glass bricks, which provide the lower levels with natural light during the day and which become sources of artificial light unto themselves by night.

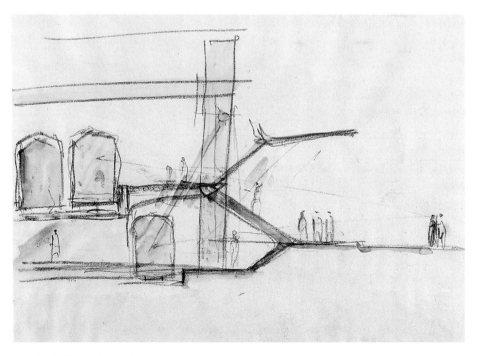

Study sketch of the roof in relation to the pedestrian walkways

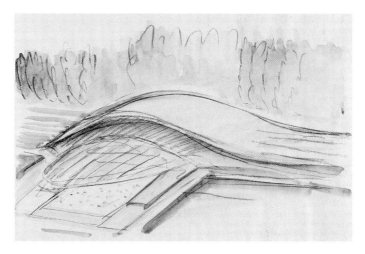

Study sketch of the roof

Scale model

Oriente Station, Lisbon, Portugal, 1993-1998

The project for Oriente Station belongs to the series of interventions planned for the city of Lisbon on the occasion of the International Exposition of 1998. The construction of a transportation hub provided the impetus to resolve a number of problems, from those of a purely infrastructural nature to the reception and distribution of Expo visitors to an age-old thorn in the city's side: the railway that had acted for so long as a physical barrier between the city and its river.

The organization of visitor and vehicular traffic being the project's central concern, the guiding principle is that of interconnection among the various parts of the complex.

The organizing element of the intervention is represented by the raised platform, 19 meters above ground level, across which the eight tracks run.

In the central part of the platform, a modular steel structure covers the area of the station, which is articulated on multiple levels. Its connection to the outside and to other transportational facilities is effectuated through a system of glazed galleries that host a number of shops and commercial activities.

The bus station is distinguished by a sequence of steel and glass canopies, each one 112 meters long and 11 meters wide, running perpendicularly to a central spine that connects the whole to the train station.

An underground station, oriented transversally with respect to the complex some 5 meters above, is set in relation to the longitudinal gallery by way of an intermediate level that hosts the ticket office.

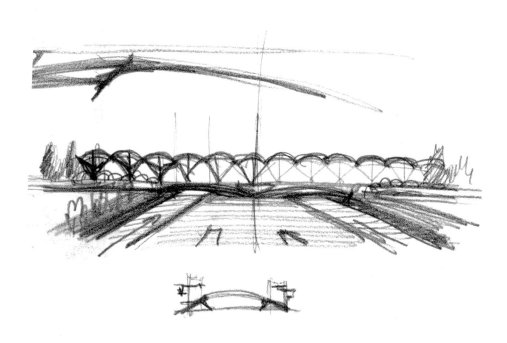

Study sketch

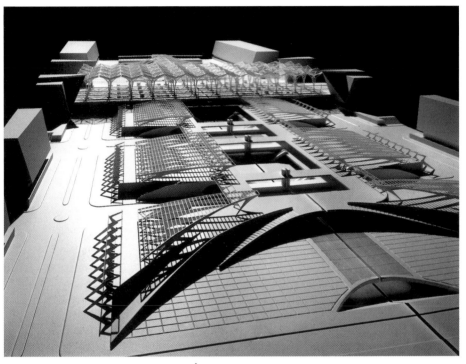

Scale model

Study sketch showing the underground station and the elevated platform

The elevated platform and the bus station

Cross section

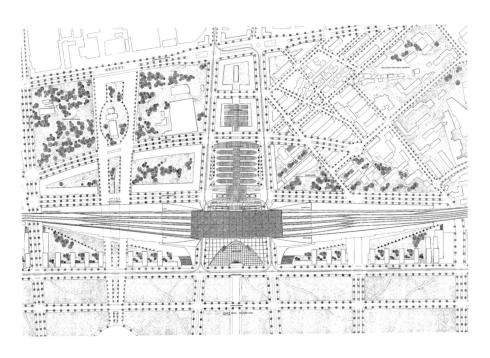

General plan

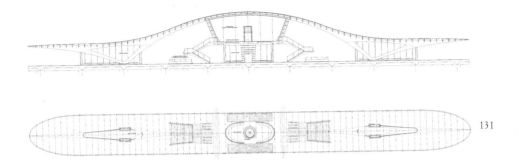

Plan and section of the platform
roofing of the bus station

View

Auditorium, Santa Cruz de Tenerife, Spain, 1991

The Santa Cruz de Tenerife Auditorium springs from the sea's edge like a free sculptural gesture, integrating a rigorous functionality with an extraordinary formal complexity, and as such constitutes a powerful architectural sign that becomes the focal point of the surrounding territory.

The structure is prevalently built of reinforced concrete, with certain elements in precompressed concrete and steel.

The main volume, created by the intersection of conical and cylindrical surfaces, rises from a stepped base that also serves as the seating area of the main auditorium which accomodates 2,000 spectators, and of a 400-seat hall for chamber music performances.

Approximately 15 meters high, the base has the function of resolving the shifts in grade between the various parts, while at the same time articulating the system of relations between the new structure and the city itself, hosting offices, rehearsal rooms, refreshment facilities, and other services. An enormous shell of reinforced concrete, its interior ceiling panelled in wood, covers the main auditorium. The 1200-seat capacity of the orchestra is augmented by a system of surrounding balconies that also serve to strengthen the inclined lateral walls.

The stage is movable, such that it can be positioned either to the fore or at the center of the auditorium.

The entrances on each side of the building are signaled by long, low arches.

The project's most striking feature is a pair of reinforced concrete wings which are supported by the south wall of the auditorium. The structure, 58 meters from base to tip, soars over the whole in a gesture of protective embrace.

132

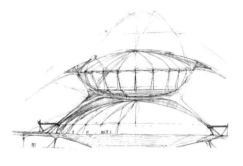

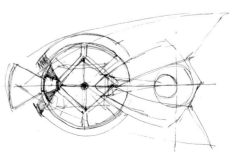

Study sketches

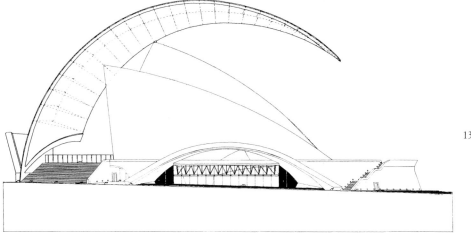

Elevation

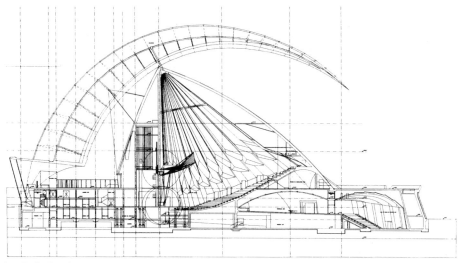

Longitudinal section

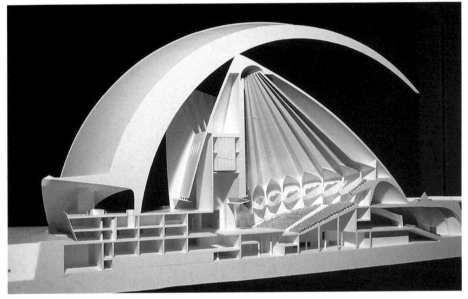

Scale model. Cross section of the auditorium

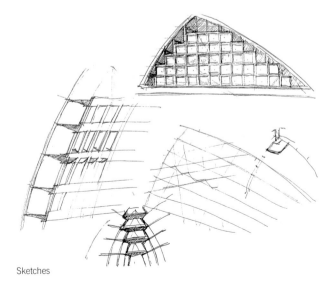

Sketches

Scale model

Exposition Center,
Santa Cruz de Tenerife, Spain,
1992-1995

The winning entry in a competition for an exposition and convention center, Calatrava's project redefines the seaward side of one of the principal access routes to the city of Santa Cruz de Tenerife.

The building is articulated on three main levels: an underground parking area (8,500 sq. m) that can be transformed into an exhibition space; a second level (3,500 sq. m) that comprises a conference hall, offices and internal services; and the vast expanse of the upper level, walled entirely in glass, which hosts the exposition hall proper and

visitor service facilities, covering an area of 12,000 square meters.

A central steel arch with a span of 142 meters is supported at each end by tripartite reinforced concrete buttresses that also serve to define the main entrances. From the principal arch hangs a secondary one that joins the two halves of the metal roof, composed of slightly curved triangular-section beams that rest at their extremities upon concrete pilasters, recalling the girded roof of the Jakem project. The cladding of the complex is prevalently in local basaltic stone.

Scale model

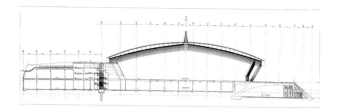

Cross section

The building under construction

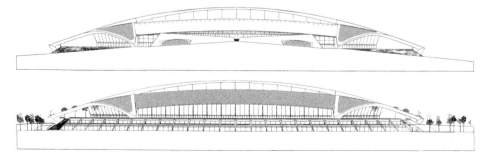

Longitudinal section and elevation

The completed building

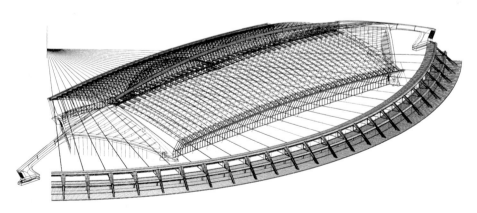

Structural scheme

Exterior views

View of the main exposition hall

Interior views

Milwaukee Art Museum,
Milwaukee, USA, 1994

This project is essentially an extension of the War Memorial Building, designed by Eero Saarinen and erected in 1957.

Particular care had to be taken to ensure that the new volumes be integrated with the landscape, and that they not interfere with the view of the lake offered by the existing buildings.

This is not to say that the relation between the existant and the new is conceived in terms of indifference, but rather of the unity and coherence of the whole.

The core of the project is an exhibition hall, exceptional for the direct visual rapport it establishes with its environs. Other distinguishing features include the lakeside facade, the suspended footbridge, the spectacular kinetic roof, and of course the original building by Saarinen.

Calatrava focused his attention on the entrance, which is connected to the rest of the complex by a raised walkway and twin ramps. Combined with the sculptural element of the roof, it creates the impression of a great winged bird coming in for a landing on the shores of Lake Michigan.

The towering glass roof over the main hall, along with the system of movable wings affixed to its spine, is the complex's most distinguishing 'territorial sign'. The movability of the wings allows one to regulate the light and temperature of the interior, indeed to completely transform its character: when closed, it reads as a covered, protected space; when open, it becomes instead a sort of vast, open-air installation in which the distinction between interior and exterior dissolves.

142

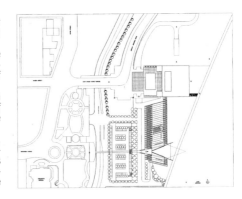

General plan

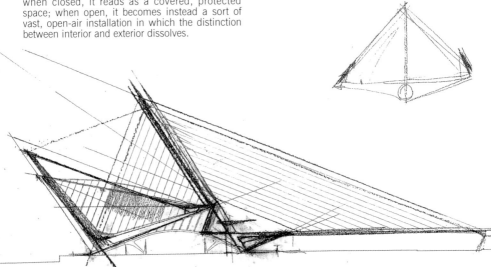

Study sketches

Scale model. The winged roof, the exhibition hall and the footbridge

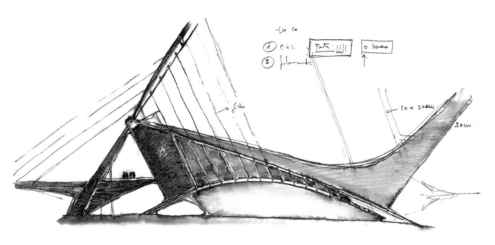

Study sketch

144

Scale model. Simulation of the movement of the central roofing element

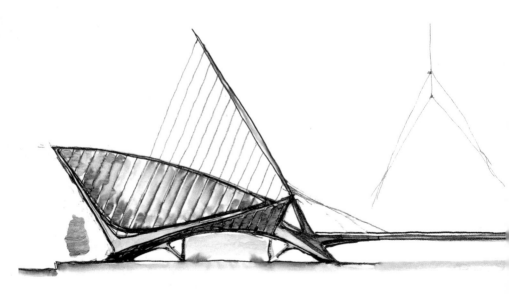

Study sketches

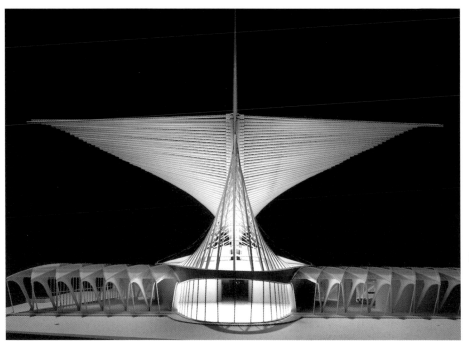

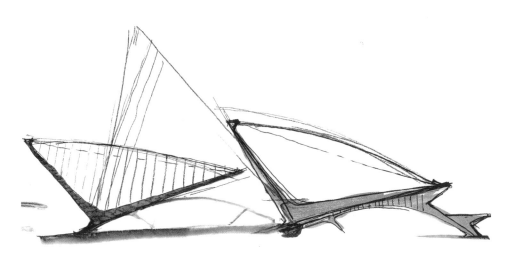

Football Stadium, Marseilles, France, 1995

In preparation for the 1998 World Cup, a competition was announced for the design of a new football stadium.

Calatrava's entry revolves around the idea of a stepped elliptical base that functions as the grandstand while also housing the service facilities and entrance gates.

The lower level beneath the grandstand is closed by a wall; from the longitudinal axes of the ellipse project two cantilevered upper grandstands supported by a system of arches reinforced by triangular elements.

The arches rest upon composite pilasters, receiving additional support from a system of buttresses that incorporate the staircases leading to the upper levels.

A circular-plan steel roof split into halves by curved girders leaves the central area occupied by the playing field open to the sky.

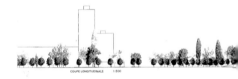

Section

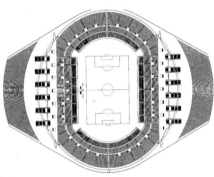

Plan

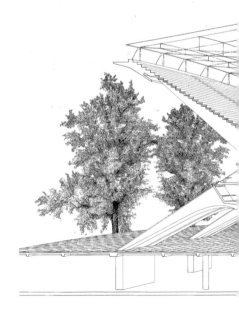

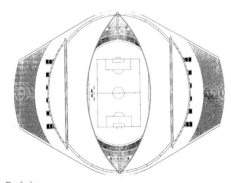

Roof plan

Perspective rendering

Scale model

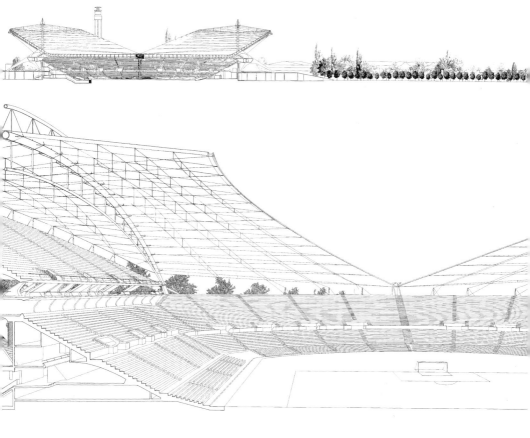

Olympya Stadium, Stockholm, 1996

To promote its candidacy for the Olympic Games of 2004, Stockholm announced a competition for the design of a new sports complex just outside the capital. The site borders the sea, immersed in the belt of wooded green that surrounds the city.

The project submitted by Calatrava operates on the premise that the insertion of the new structures be effectuated with maximum respect for the natural enviroment, and provides for the partial dismantling of the complex once the Games are over. The new project encompasses the entire area of Hammarby Waterfront, and is aimed at establishing both functional and symbolic connections with the city.

The Olympia Stadium, situated in a hilly area adjacent to the waterfront, is covered by a longitudinal structure of depressed arches in steel, wood and glass exceptional for its transparency and lightness of weight. Below is a concrete base articulated on two levels.

The distinguishing feature of the roof lies in the fact that it opens and closes, thanks to the rotatory movement of the the two elements of which it is composed. Designed to remain open during the Games, it can then be closed afterwards.

Furthermore, the dimensions of the stadium can be reduced, insofar as certain components are designed to be easily dismantled, removed and used toward other ends.

Included in the overall project is another, smaller stadium to be built nearby the Olympya. Intended primarily as a practice field for the duration of the Games, it will be dismantled upon their conclusion.

Scale model

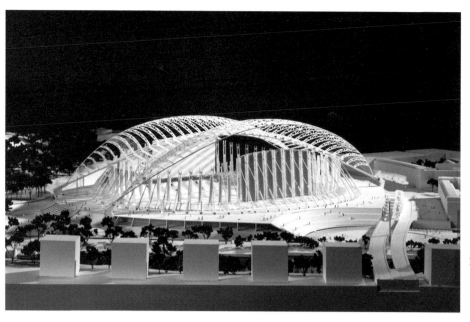

Scale models demonstrating the movement of the roof

"City of Science" Cultural Complex, Valencia, Spain, 1991

The project for the "City of Science" is part of a vast program of urban renewal designated for an area outside the city center along the river Turia, a program whose specifications were outlined in an architectural competition that saw Calatrava as the winner.

The point of departure for the project is a stretch of the river, and its main objective is the organic definition of the riverfront. Three new structures were originally planned to be erected along its banks – the Museum of Science and Technology, the Planetarium, and a telecommunications tower – all of them interconnected through a system of public spaces articulated on several levels. In order to realize the project, it will be necessary to divert automobile traffic from the area.

In a later version of the project, the telecommunications tower was replaced by an arts center.

The Museum of Science and Technology is configured like a huge, glass-sheathed exposition hall. Rectangular in plan and set atop an elevated base, the museum is perched directly at water's edge. The expansive interior space is generated by the repetition of the transverse section, notable for its height. The lower level consists in a structure of reinforced concrete, and the ample space above is distinguished by the presence of a series of massive girders that assume the form of arches.

Seven levels of platforms are disposed along the northern facade. A system of vertical connections organizes these spaces, which are designed to accomodate thematic exhibitions.

The Planetarium is an elliptical-plan shell sustained by arches composed of movable and fixed metal elements; contained within this shell is the concrete hemisphere of the planetarium itself.

150

Scale model showing the new bridge, the museum, the Planeta

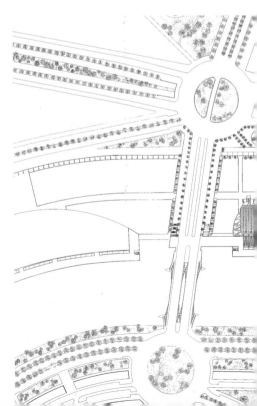

General plan

he Arts center

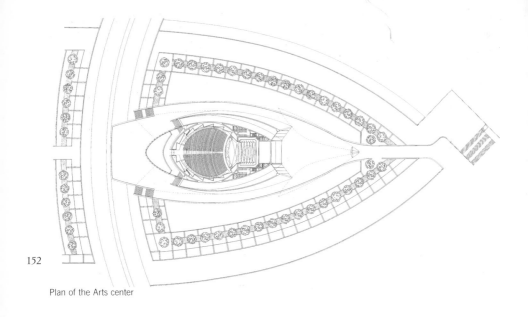

Plan of the Arts center

Scale model of the Arts center

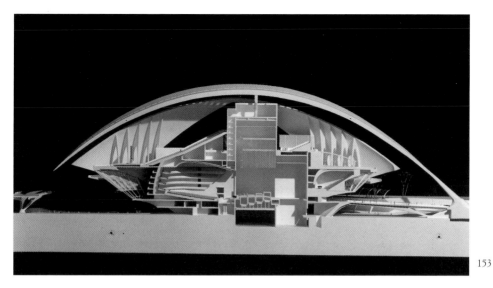

Longitudinal section of the Arts center

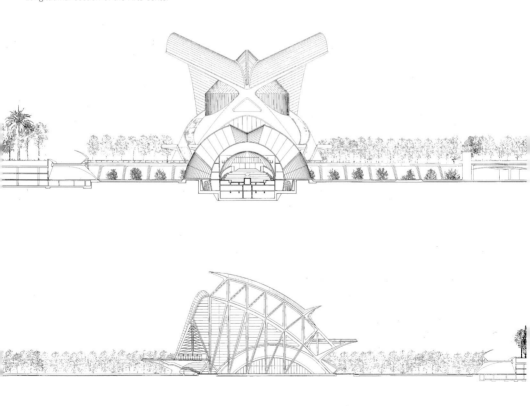

Sections of the first version of the project

Planetarium. Relation between the central hemisphere and the exterior shell

Planetarium. Main entrance

Planetarium. Detail of the exterior shell

The Bridges

The construction of a bridge has always gone hand in hand with the will to inscribe a powerful architectural sign upon the surrounding territory.

Along with the fact that a bridge carries an inherent symbolic value, the centuries have demonstrated that bridge design, as well as the building process itself, have always been a natural laboratory for testing, verifying and transcending the current technological and material paradigms of a given epoch.

Since the early 1980s, Calatrava's *corpus* has proven itself to be both a natural and heterodox continuation of the work of some of the greatest engineers of our century, from Freyssenet and Eiffel to Maillart and Morandi.

The bridge, for Calatrava, is meant to be interpreted as a monumental presence, a signal that constructs new relationships with its environs. His insistence on whiteness for every last surface, aside from deftly resolving the technical problem of long-term protection, intensifies the perception of the

"Designing a bridge is in a way an exercise in the esthetics of engineering, and for this reason I believe that greater attention should be dedicated to the integration of esthetics and technology. In my view, the construction of a bridge requires a particular kind of architectural sensitivity from an engineer, especially when imagining its form, which can be conceived as an important point of reference, a note of interest in a landscape otherwise devoid of any distinctive character".

(Santiago Calatrava, 1997)

structure as an element of order with respect to the natural and urban environment.

In his more than sixty bridge designs, realized from 1979 to the present, Calatrava has addressed all of the traditional typologies (suspension, truss, pylon, arch, et.al.), working with subtle variations on the theme that often seem to become a visual dramatization of the central engineering principle of the typology in question. His complex use of geometry, his unique marriage of technology and formal vision, and his constant recourse to movement render many of these projects *provocations* directed against the conventions and repetitions of traditional bridge design and construction.

The sculptural quality of Calatrava's bridges is the fruit of his constant artistic and technical research, in which the study of the object in physical space on the one hand and of pure form on the other interpenetrate, enriching one another immeasurably.

Caballeros Bridge, Lerida, Spain, 1984, project

Footbridge over the Segre River
Overall length 210 m
Maximum span 140 m
Height of pylon 28 m
Height over the river 7 m

A competition entry, this bridge was designed for a site outside the ancient walls of Lerida, where it would have connected the city nucleus, by way of the Calle de los Caballeros, to a green area on the other side of the Segre River.

The vertical bearing element rises from the firm ground of the higher of the river's banks, on the same side as the city center. The pylon, a geometrically complex steel structure that cantilevers out over the water, rests on a compound reinforced concrete base set on piles.

Nine cables part from the top of the pylon to sustain the footbridge, which is covered by an aluminum canopy; another seven cables fan out to meet the curved portico structure that anchors them, which, together with the staircase that descends to the riverbank, characterizes the bridgehead. Two symmetrical ramps provide access on the opposite bank.

160

Scale model

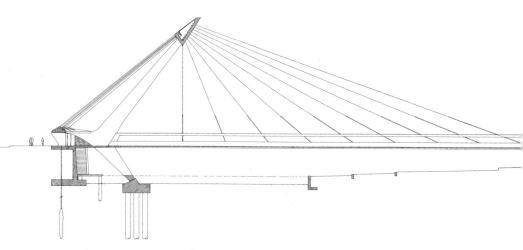

Longitundinal section

Scale model

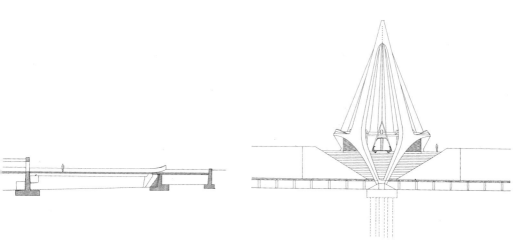

Elevation of the bridgehead with cross section of the footbridge

Felipe II – Bach de Roda Bridge, Barcelona, Spain, 1984, built 1986-1987

Automobile and pedestrian railroad overpass
Commissioned by the Unità Operativa de
Projectes Urbans of the city of Barcelona
Overall length 129 m
Central span 46 m
Height of arch 10 m
Height above tracks 8 m

Barcelona's candidacy for the 1992 Olympic Games was the impetus around which a series of urban planning initiatives were undertaken. Aimed for the most part at rehabilitating the peripheral areas, they led to the realization of numerous interventions that would significantly change the face of the city.

The Bach de Roda bridge is one such intervention. The length of the bridge arches ever so slightly to gain the necessary height over the railway line, which it crosses at an oblique angle. The central span is sustained by four steel arches: the two main ones stand vertically and are set upon pylons of reinforced concrete clad in granite; the secondary arches, connected to the main ones along the top of the curve by triangular braces, are inclined at a 30° angle. Their reinforced concrete feet stablize the structure laterally.

Cables drop from the arches to sustain the bridge-beams, which are composed of box girders crossed by the steel trusses that support the concrete slab of the carriageway.

In the central part of the bridge the external border of the pedestrian walkway is defined by the line along which the suspension cables that descend from the secondary arches are anchored. This solution creates a widening of the walkway, effectively transforming it into an observation platform that is slightly raised with respect to the level of the carriageway.

Four staircases are incorporated into the buttresses that absorb the thrust of the secondary arches, thereby providing access from the bridge to the unused areas on either side of the train tracks, which the city is planning to convert into a park.

162

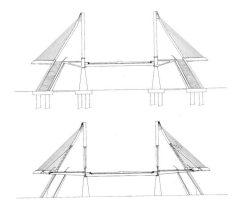

Cross sections

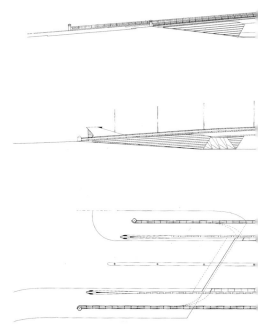

Elevation, longitudinal section, plan

The staircase leading to the area beneath the bridge

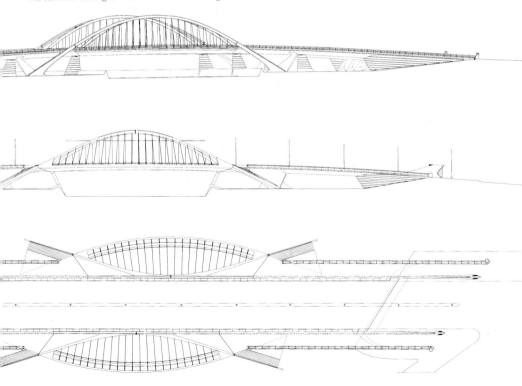

View of the completed project

The staircase, the pedestrian walkway, the road

9 de Octubre Bridge, Valencia, Spain, 1986, built 1987-1989

Automobile and pedestrian bridge
over the Turia River
Commissioned by the City of Valencia
Overall length 144 m
Width 50 m
Height from foundation 4.9 m

The typology here is that of the "twin" bridge, a double viaduct, symmetrical with respect to its longitudinal axis. This "duplication" serves, on the one hand, to conserve the image of the boulevard of which the bridge is an extension, and on the other to lighten the structure, insofar as an ample void is opened up between the two carriageways.

Spanning the dry bed of the Turia River, the bridge acts as a "hydraulic metaphor" by recalling the form of navigable locks and by evoking, with the gently undulations that characterize the lateral containment walls, the water that once flowed here.

The concrete bridge-beams are supported by trapezoidal reinforced concrete piers set a 7.2-meter intervals along the inside edges of the carriageways; at corresponding intervals along the outside edges are gracefully tapered steel columns, which confer to the bridge an attitude of lightness that is usually associated with structures built according to the principle of tensile stress.

Cantilevering out from the main structure, 40 cm above the level of the carriageway, are the prefabricated concrete pedestrian platforms. The fact that these walkways are detached allows additional light to illuminate the space beneath the bridge, thus accentuating yet further the impression of suspension and lightness.

The tapered steel braces that connect the walkways to the main structure repeat the form of the pilasters mentioned above.

Rough plywood forms were used for all the poured concrete work, including the diagonal ribs beneath the bridge-beams.

Four ramps, two at each end of the bridge, provide access to the riverbanks, allowing for the eventual use of the space beneath the bridge, which Calatrava has designed with the same care dedicated to the rest of the structure.

The bridgeheads are marked by monumental concrete piers crowned by steel sculptures in the form of a talon which also serve as sources of illumination.

166

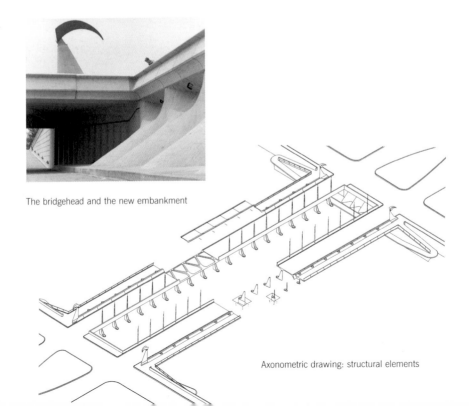

The bridgehead and the new embankment

Axonometric drawing: structural elements

View from the riverbed

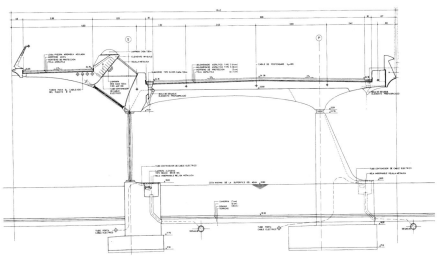

Cross section

Alamillo Bridge, Seville, 1987-1992

Automobile and pedestrian bridge over the Guadalquivir River
Commissioned by the Junta de Andalucia
Overall length 250 m
Central span 200 m
Suspension bridge with inclined pylon (32°)
Height of pylon from carriageway 142 m

The project for the Alamillo bridge is part of a more extensive program of infrastructural interventions commissioned in preparation for the 1992 Expo and aimed at facilitating communication between the cities in immediate proximity to Seville. In fact, the project proposed by Calatrava also included another, identical bridge, positioned inversely with respect to the Alamillo (never realized), as well as a viaduct (see p. 175) that traverses the island of Cartuja.

The Alamillo project represents a variation on the theme of the suspension bridge. A dramatically asymmetrical inclined mast sustains the central span through a system of cables, a solution that allows the elimination of the posterior cables that would be necessary in a conventional suspension bridge. Calatrava had already investigated this structural principle in his *Running Torso* sculpture of 1986.

The resultant of the stresses at the base of the mast is vertical; horizontal thrusts that may be caused by wind are easily absorbed by the structure. The mast itself is composed of hollow, hexagonal-section steel elements reinforced with concrete.

In the original plan the mast was to have been constructed entirely of reinforced concrete, with the suspension cables placed in position one by one as the structure grew. The contractor, however, preferred another method whereby steel elements balanced by counterweights were gradually added as each cable was anchored to the central span, finally arriving at the point where the pylon's height and weight were enough to sustain the whole.

As for the bridge-beams, a hexagonal-section box girder constitutes the spine, to which the 13 pairs of cables emanating from the pylon are anchored; welded to either side of this central girder are the lightweight crossbeams that support the two cantilevered carriageways.

The top side of the box girder, 3.75 meters wide, becomes an elevated walkway, 1.6 meters above the road surface.

The viaduct that crosses the island of Cartuja, originally designed to connect the Alamillo bridge to its twin, is a double-tiered system of cantilevered platforms: from a sequence of symmetrical inclined pylons in reinforced concrete project, on the upper level, two vehicular carriageways, while directly beneath run two pedestrian walkways. Seen in cross section, the space underneath the viaduct assumes the form of a vault traversed by a triple series of circular openings that illuminate the porticoed area defined by the pylons, conceived as a transitional space between a parking lot and the entrance to the Expo.

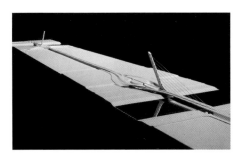

Scale model

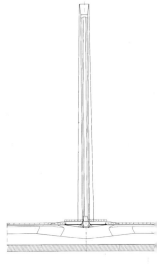

Elevations

Scale model

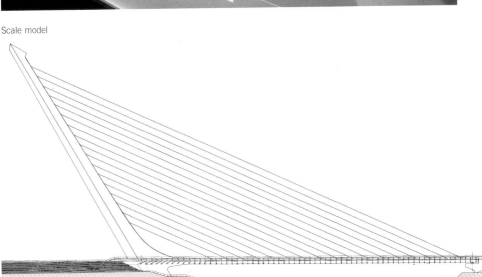

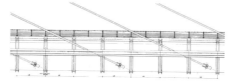

Cross section of the bridge-beams

The building site

The completed bridge

The underside of the Alamillo Bridge

The Cartuja viaduct

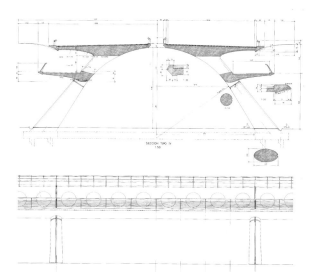

Cartuja viaduct: cross section and elevation

Cascine Bridge, Florence, Italy, 1987, project

Footbridge over the Arno River
Overall length 125 m
Central span 74 m
Height of arch 10 m
Height from river 21 m

This project for a footbridge over the Arno was designed for the 17th Milan Triennial as part of an initiative that called for the elaboration of new architectural interventions in nine Italian cities.

Calatrava proposed a footbridge that links Le Cascine park with area of Monte Uliveto.

A sinuously sculptural arched structure rises from four reinforced concrete buttresses, each of which incorporates a staircase that connects the walkway to the banks of the Arno.

Continuing the line of the arch and absorbing its thrust, the buttresses bifurcate to allow the pedestrian platform – suspended in its central span and sustained by the embankments at its extremes – to pass through uninterrupted.

The suspended platform beneath the arch has an elliptical plan and is stiffened by trusses disposed radially with respect to the longitudinal axis. The arch and the bridge-beams are made of steel.

176

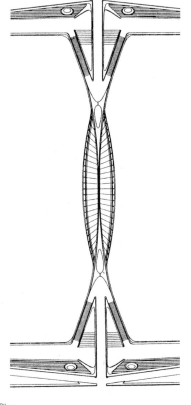

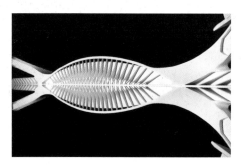

Scale model

Plan

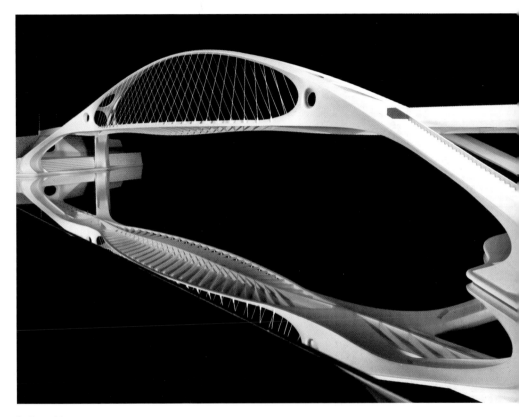

Scale model

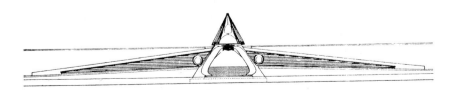

Cross section

Wettstein Bridge, Basel, Switzerland, 1988, project

Automobile and pedestrian bridge
over the Reno River
Overall length 199 m
Maximum span 66 m
Height of arch 6 m

The reconstruction of the Wettstein bridge offered Calatrava the opportunity to engage in a formal and technical discourse with the original, a truss bridge built in 1879, of which there remain two oblong masonry pylons. Momentarily suspending his ongoing experiments with "mixed" construction, the architect proposed a structure entirely in steel.

The new bridge, to paraphrase an observation by Kenneth Frampton, seems to rest on the pylons as if they weren't there at all, with an attitude that simultaneously expresses the celebration of a tradition and its outright rejection.

This statement was surely motivated by an analysis of the bridge's structure, which seems at first a straightforward lattice girder system, but which in reality is a complex spatial web whose dimensions and direction change continually.

Furthering the impression of lightness is the fact that the whole structure is supported at just eight points, which it perches upon almost as if on tiptoe.

At the formal level, the welded steel underside of the bridge can be read as an arch, but in terms of structure it is an integral part of the system of posts and braces that supports the central carriageway and the two cantilevered, slightly detached pedestrian walkways on each side.

The cleats that constitute the eight points of contact are single blocks of steel anchored by cables, capping the existing pylons with supreme sculptural elegance. The distribution of stress among the various elements both stiffens the bridge and permits a significant reduction of the structure's mass and weight.

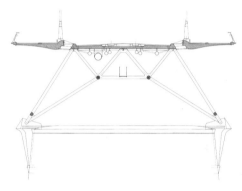

Cross section of the point where the bridge meets the pylon

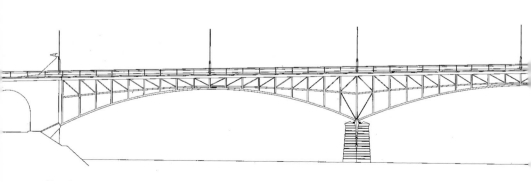

Elevation

Scale model

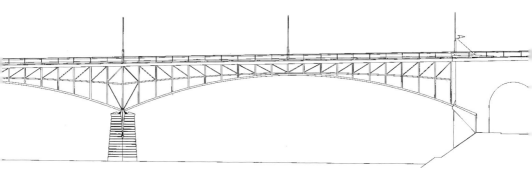

Lusitania Bridge, Merida, Spain, 1988, built 1990-1991

Automobile and pedestrian bridge over
the Guadiana River
Overall length 465 m
Central span 189 m
Lateral spans 144 m
Interval between pylons (lateral spans) 45 m
Height of arch 34 m

The Lusitania bridge belongs to that category of works that succeed in establishing, and not for their dimensions alone, a relationship of scale with the landscape that is at once monumental and poetic.

Situated 600 meters downriver from an ancient Roman bridge, the Lusitania was conceived to create a "harmonic contrast" with the older structure, to complement it rather than overwhelm it. Yet Calatrava does not by any means renounce the possibility of marking the slightly hilly territory of Merida with a potent visual element, perceptible even from great distances.

The bridge is composed of three parts: the arch that sustains the central span and the two lateral tracts, held up by pylons. From both a structural and syntactical point of view, this adoption of two different systems of support, indeed of two different bridge typologies, implies the existence of points of caesura.

The box girder that constitutes the longitudinal spine of the structure is the project's main element of continuity, a quality that is maintained in cross section as well, inasmuch as the two cantilevered carriageways run unaltered and unobstructed for the bridge's entire length.

The central bearing element of the bridge is the aforementioned box girder, which is composed of prefabricated sections of reinforced concrete and has a constant height of 4.45 meters.

During construction, the girder was held up by temporary supports which were removed once the weight of the central span had been transferred to the arch.

The arch sustains its load by way of 23 pairs of steel cables and is stabilized by reinforced concrete saddles whose task it is to absorb the load of the bridge-beams before accepting the arch. The slab of the carriageways is supported by hollow wings of precompressed concrete which cantilever out from the central box girder. This structural solution creates a nearly uninterrupted fissure between the girder and the carriageways, a continuous line of light and air that not only reduces the weight of the platforms but encourages a delicate play of light and shadow on the flanks of the main beam.

A pedestrian and bicycle platform, 5.5 meters wide, runs down the center of the bridge along the top of the longitudinal girder at a height of 1.5 meters with respect to the road surface on either side; portals are cut into the saddles of the arch to allow its passage.

This platform is defined laterally by a railing, as well as by the sequence of cables that descend from the arch, forking out from a single point to then find purchase on both sides of the box girder.

This solution is rendered possible by the unusual section of the arch, an inverted triangle composed of three tubular elements stiffened by a system of vertical and diagonal braces; the suspension cables part from the lower of the three.

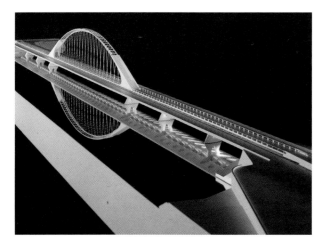

Scale model

View of the bridge

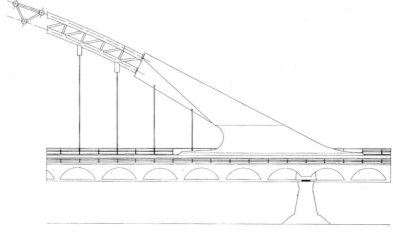

Elevation: detail of the base of the arch

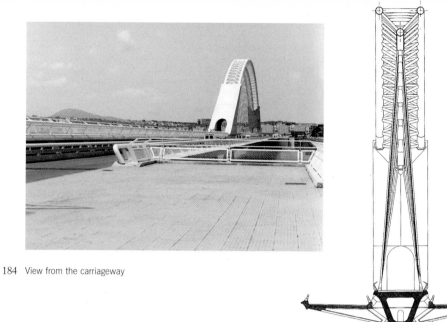

184 View from the carriageway

Cross section

The underside of the bridge

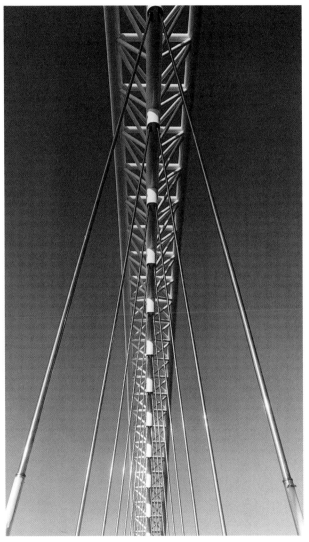

The arch and suspension cables

La Devesa Bridge,
Ripoll, Spain, 1989,
built 1990-1991

Footbridge over the Ter River
Commissioned by the Municipality of Ripoli
Overall length 65 m
Maximum span 44 m
Height of arch 6.5 m

The bridge ingeniously resolves the 5-meter-drop in grade from one bank of the river Ter to the other, while at the same time fulfilling the function of opening up communication between the center of town, the train station and the La Devesa area, for which future development is planned.

The bridge's equilibrium derives from the combined use of diverse static systems.

The structure of the bridge is characterized by a steel arch that leans outward at a 25° angle, and a ribbed walkway paved in wood. The arch parts from the existing embankment wall and is met on the other side by a concrete pylon that follows its line; the load of the walkway is transferred to the arch by braces that also serve to stiffen the structure.

Since the arch is inclined, and therefore the braces as well, these latter must bear both the horizontal and the vertical thrust of the load, meaning that for all practical purposes they must maintain a state of pure tensile stress in order for the arch to function as such.

Because the loads are eccentric with respect to the plane of the arch, there is the risk that the walkway might twist: this problem is resolved by the introduction of a heavy circular-section girder that resists torsion and distributes the contrary forces to the bases of the arch.

Scale model of the first version

View from La Devesa

The underside of the staircase, the concrete pylon, the tubular girder
and the bridgehead on the opposite bank

The arch

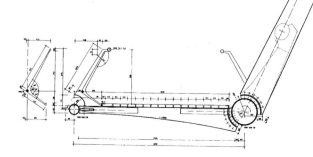

Cross section at the point of the arch's maximum height

Puerto Bridge, Ondarroa, Spain, 1989-1995

Automobile and pedestrian bridge on the Artibay River
Commissioned by the Municipality of Ondarroa
Overall length 71.5 m
Maximum span 71.5 m
Height of arch 15 m

The bridge spans the Artibay River at its confluence with the waters of Ondarroa's port. The decision to place it here grew out of the dual need to accomodate an increase in the port's activities and to relieve the city center of the traffic problems caused by inadequate vehicular communication between the two sides of the river.

The project also creates a new pedestrian route between the two banks and offers the possibility of access to the water's edge.

The structure of the bridge is characterized by an asymmetrical arch whose incline defines the truncated ellipse form of the opening that separates the two platforms, one for vehicular and one for pedestrian traffic. The carriageway, perfectly straight and horizontal, is supported by a box girder whose extremities rest on the embankments, while the walkway, slightly arched and bowed, is cantilevered.

From the vertical arch descend the paired suspension cables that define the internal edge of the carriageway, as do the inclined braces which, together with a sequence of struts welded to the box girder, sustain the raised pedestrian walkway and define its curve.

Staircases provide access to the space beneath the bridge. The opening between the two platforms, rhythmically measured out by structural elements, generates a suggestive play of light and shadow.

View from the carriageway

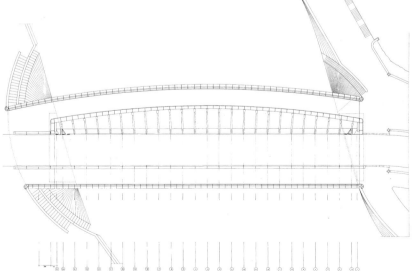

Plan

View from the port

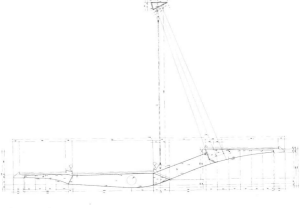

Cross section

East London Crossing, London, Great Britain, 1990, project

Automobile and pedestrian bridge over the Thames River
Commissioned by a private interest
Overall length 630 m
Distance between the two pylons 510 m
Span of arch over the bridge-beams 200 m
Height of arch over carriageway 25 m
Total height of arch 103 m
Width 35 m

Conceived as a link between Thamesmead and Beckton, had it been built the East London Crossing would have represented not only a vital infrastructural element but a world-class landmark for the capital. But the colossal dimensions of the structure, due to the width of the river and the requisite that ships be able to pass beneath, created difficulties in its being accepted as a feasible project, even if a good deal of its planning was dedicated expressly to methods and management of all the phases of construction. The fact that only two footings had to be built, thus rendering it relatively economical, was not enough to win approval.

The structure of the bridge-beams consists in a hollow box girder that runs the entire length of the bridge, from which project transverse steel trusses that support the concrete carriageway slabs. While the lateral spans are sustained by pylons, the central span of 200 meters is suspended from a steel arch that splits the six-lane carriageway longitudinally in symmetrical three-lane halves. The V-shaped supports from which the arch springs are formally similar to that used in the the La Devesa bridge in Ripoli, though they operate according to different principles.

These 'V's bear both the load of the carriageway and the thrust of the arch. Seen in terms of statics, the fact that they are anchored to footings and connected to vertical pylons makes them not unlike lattice girders on an enormous scale. They transfer the thrust of the arch to riverbed footings and are stabilized by the action of the vertical pylons.

The points at which the arch intercepts the bridge-beams are designed in such a way as to avoid excessive thrust being transmitted to the pylons. The element that links the carriageway with the apex of the arch has a structural role of primary importance: that one touch of rigidity in an otherwise fluid design serves to stabilize the arch and to impede lateral flexing and deformations, and as such it represents yet another step in Calatrava's research on the deformation of the arch.

Had the bridge been built, the main phases of construction would have been the setting of the underwater footings, the erection of the pylons and lateral carriageways (reinforced concrete platforms supported by ribs affixed to the central box girder), and finally the positioning of the central tract, which would have been transported by ship.

194

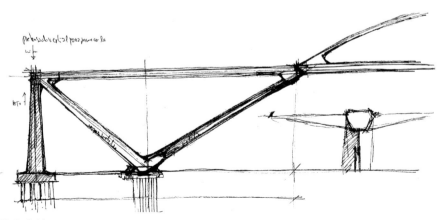

Study sketch

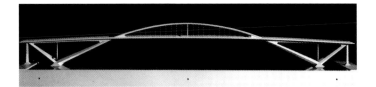

Scale model

Photomontage

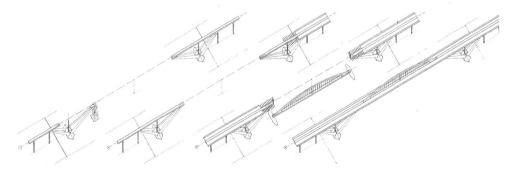

Axonometric drawing showing the phases of construction

Bridge and Subway Station, Alameda, Valencia, Spain, 1991-1995

Automobile and pedestrian bridge
over the Turia River
Commissioned by the Generalitat di Valencia
Overall length 163 m
Maximum span 130 m
Height of arch 14 m

For a site on the now dry bed of the Turia River, Calatrava designed three structures which jointly define a new public space: a multi-level underground subway station situated perpendicularly with respect to the river's course, an open plaza, and a bridge.

Since the entire complex was built simultaneously, in order to avoid excessive congestion on the construction site, the bridge was assembled elsewhere and then set in place once the station and plaza were completed.

The subway station, configured with one central waiting platform and two lateral ones and thus able to accomodate four trains, is covered by a complex ribbed structure in exposed, white-pigmented concrete which rests either directly on the lateral walls or on struts projecting from them.

In the central stretch of the station, these walls are perforated by openings that endow the underground structure with natural light and ventilation.

The entrances to the station from the plaza above are distinguished by a system of movable "doors" that act as roofing elements when closed.

The structure of the 130-meter central span of the bridge is composed of an inclined arch (20°) supported by two reinforced concrete pillars set approximately 15 meters in from the river's edge, while the short lateral spans are sustained by the embankments.

The slightly curved bridge-beams, entirely in steel, consist in a box girder that runs the entire length of the bridge; the structure is stiffened and stabilized by the wideness of the girder, which is composed of four hollow cells, and by the action of the cantilevered pedestrian platforms, which are joined to the girder by transverse trusses.

The compound profile of the arch is created from the union of two hollow beams of different form (one triangular in section, the other circular) and constant diameter, held together by welded steel inserts. In order to ensure the stability that is potentially threatened by the lean of the arch, flexion-resistant steel braces are placed at intervals of 5.84 meters; these also serve to transfer the load of the central span to the arch.

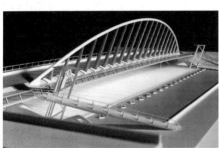

Scale model. The bridge and the plaza

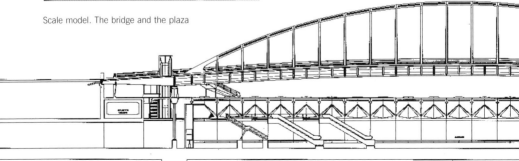

Longitudinal section. The bridge and the subway station below

The completed project

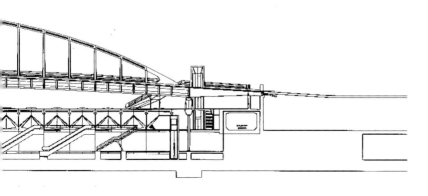

The bridge

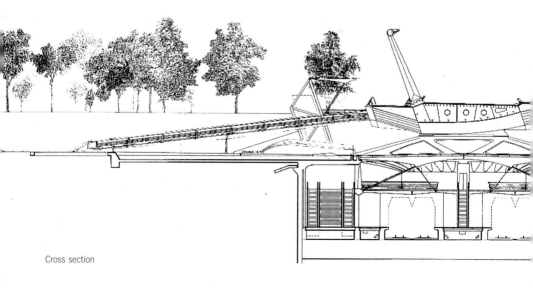

Cross section

The interior of the station

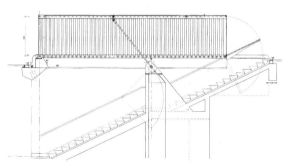

Detail of the station's entrance stairway

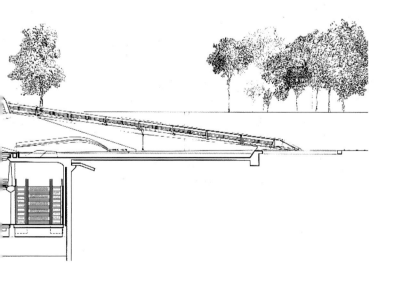

Médoc Bridge, Bordeaux, France, 1991, project

Automobile and pedestrian swing bridge
over the Garonne River
Overall length 416 m
Central element in two spans of 120 m each
Height of tower 100 m
Height above water 20 m (avg)

The competition staged by the Direction des Services Tecniques of the city of Bordeaux called for the design of a bridge that would be the centerpiece of a revitalization campaign for an urban area along the Garonne.

The specific aim was that of establishing an efficient link between the center of the city and the outlying areas in the course of development.

One of the main requisites was that the structure should not impede maritime traffic, which led Calatrava to come up with the idea of a rotating suspension bridge.

An X-section steel pole rises from an underwater footing in reinforced concrete.

A system of paired cables anchored to this vertical load-bearing element sustains the central span, while the slightly bowed pedestrian platforms cantilever out on a system of triangular braces attached at the top to the cables and at the bottom to the carriageway.

As in nearly all of Calatrava's bridges, the "psychological priority" of the pedestrian is ensured by elevating the walkway, both literally and metaphorically, above the level of the road; the difference in grade between the two levels reaches a maximum of three meters in the bridge's central tract.

This solution reveals itself to be equally generous with regard to both pedestrians and motorists, for neither is impeded in any way from enjoying a full view of the river.

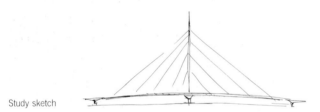

Study sketch

Photomontage

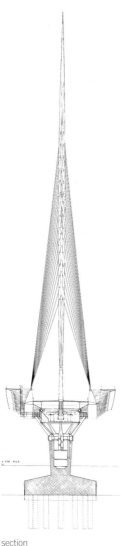

Cross section

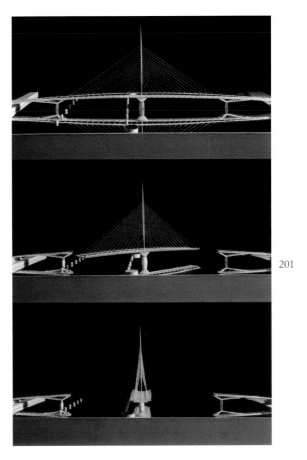

Scale model: from closed to open

Cross section of the lateral spans

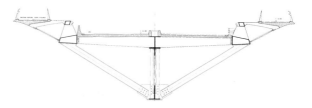

Cross section of the central span

Solferino Bridge, Paris, France, 1992, project

Footbridge over the Seine River
Overall length 130 m
Central span 76 m

The Solferino bridge is at once an ample observation deck over the Seine and an efficacious shortcut from the area of the Louvre to that of the Quai d'Orsay on the opposite bank.

Born of a competition held by the Etablissement Public du Grand Louvre, it seems to construct its image on the basis of the venerable tradition of metal bridges, but in reality its system of support introduces unconventional new solutions.

The bridge is distinguished by the fact that each individual brace transmits the load of the platform to the three-dimensional arches at a different angle. It is also unusual in that the walkway is divided into two lateral platforms with a wider, slightly elevated central course.

This central course is paved with slabs of tranlucent marble which allow one to see the complex geometry of the structure below, while the lateral walkways are finished in wood.

At night, a subtly designed system of artificial illumination transforms the central course into an ephemeral carpet of light.

The entire structure rests upon two perpendicular steel pontoons anchored to underwater footings of reinforced concrete.

As elsewhere, Calatrava never considers the space beneath a bridge as a marginal aspect of the project, and indeed he continues here to completely expose the structure and to interpret dry engineering principles as elements of formal beauty, whether it be the abstract pattern of the bridge's structural underbelly, the elegant curve of the bearing arches or the sculptural form of the footings.

The north embankment incorporates a complex system of staircase-ramps which provide access to the various levels of the riverbank and also conduct to a vaulted space that houses the entrance to an underground passageway connected with the Louvre. This entrance can be sealed off by a door consisting in a motorized system of articulated rods whose form and movement recall that of an eye.

Photomontages

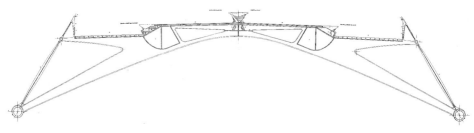

Cross section

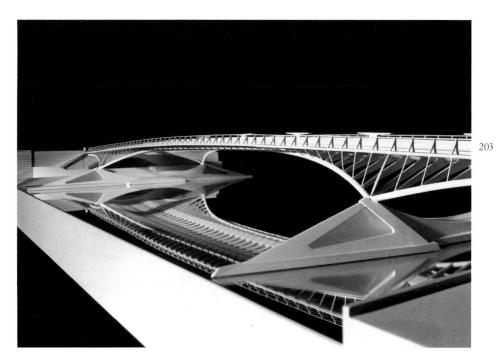

Scale model

Ile Falcon Bridge, Sierre, Switzerland, 1993, project

Vehicular bridge over the Rhone River
Overall length 684 m
Maximum span 135 m

A viaduct in the Rhone valley was the theme of the competition for which Calatrava designed this double-arch bridge that posed the challenge of having to obey the curve of the existing road. One of the project's distinguishing features derives from the separation of the two carriageways, which serves to both lighten the structure and reduce the area of shadow projected by the bridge onto the water's surface.

The fact that the bridge is decidedly longer than strictly necessary for crossing the river is owed to the architect's careful quest to reduce the number of support pylons, thereby minimizing any interference that the new structure might create with regard to the natural environment.

Two pairs of steel arches stiffened by crossbraces issue from a single central pylon, diverging as they proceed toward the extremities to meet pylons situated on either side of the twin carriageway.

The bridge-beams, composed of steel box girders, transfer their weight to the arches by way of steel cables anchored to the internal edges of the carriageways.

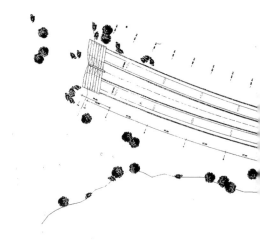

Plan

Photomontages

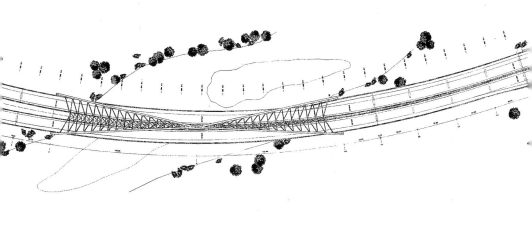

Trinity Bridge, Salford, Manchester, Great Britain, 1993-1995

Footbridge over the Irwell River
Commissioned by the Phoenix Initiative
and the City of Salford
Overall length 78.5 m
Maximum span 54 m
Height of pylon 41 m
Diameter of mast 55-122 cm

This spectacular footbridge connects the city of Salford with neighboring Manchester, its marked pitch compensating for the difference in grade between the two sides of the Irwell River, and represents a further step in the architect's experimentation with the asymmetrical suspension bridge and the leaning mast.

Access to the bridge on the Salford side is provided by a centrally situated staircase and a pair of curved ramps that eventually merge to form a single pedestrian platform 4 meters wide and 67 meters long.

The structure of the gently arched tract spanning the river consists in a torsion-resistant, triangular-section box girder which is supported by cables fanning out from a tapered steel mast that leans with precarious majesty back toward the stair and ramps; a reinforced concrete pier supports it from below.

Also noteworthy is the high degree of detail in the system of cleats by which the cables are anchored to the mast.

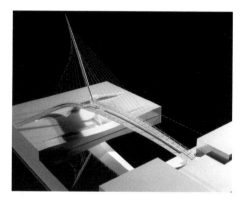

Scale model

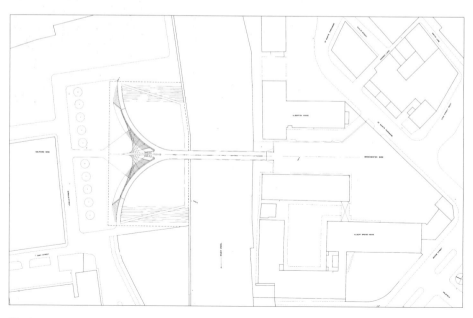

Site plan

The completed bridge

Access from the Salford side

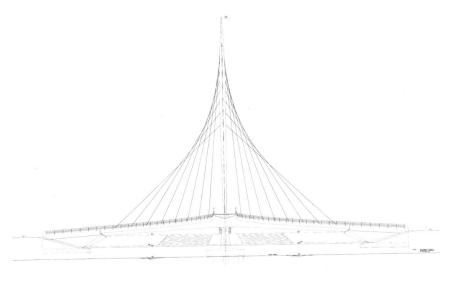

Cross section

View from beneath the bridgehead

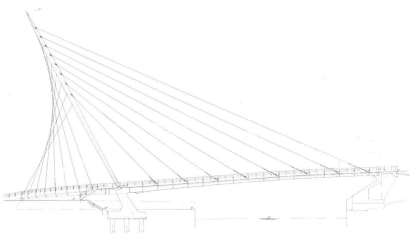

Longitudinal section

Quay Point Bridge, Bristol, Great Britain, 1994, project

Overall length 64 m
Maximum span 64 m

Projecting abutments support a doubly bifurcated arch structure, beneath which extends a slightly bowed pedestrian walkway with a translucent pavement.
 A transparent, movable canopy flares out from either side of the arch.

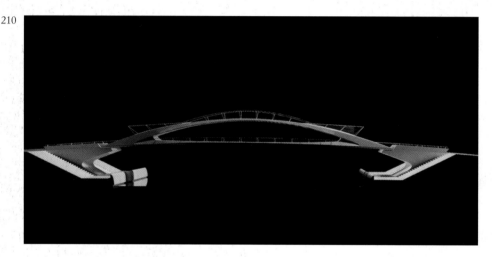

Scale model

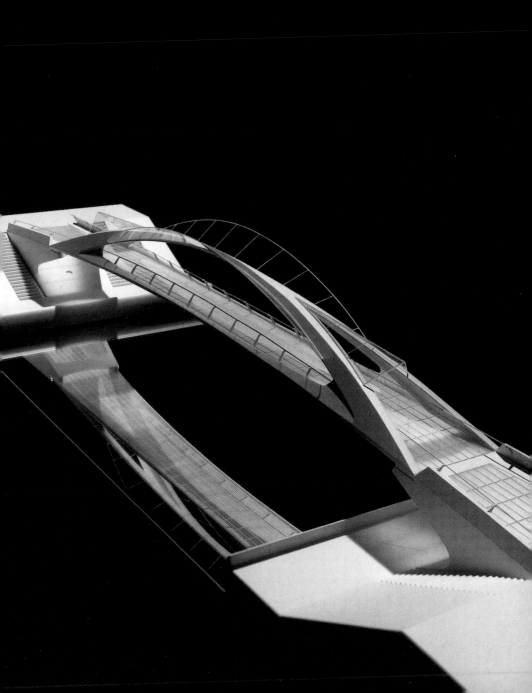

Port of Barcelona, Barcelona, Spain, 1997, project

The idea of building a bridge at the mouth of the Port of Barcelona is motivated by the desire for an element which, in both its form and placement, might lend a defining touch to the port of this ambitious city, which has long been implementing an massive program of urban renewal and rehabilitation.

The new bridge offers itself as a gateway, a threshold between the protected harbor and the open sea, signalling access to the port on the one hand, inviting the possibility of new relationships and further expansions on the other.

The fact that the bridge must not obstruct the passage of large ships and that it must cover the not inconsiderable span of 175 meters led the architect to come up with two feasible solutions: a bascule bridge composed of two elements, each one approximately 60-80 meters long, and a swing bridge, again of two elements, each more than 100 meters long.

In the first case, the repercussions regarding the utilization of the moles are minimal, since the footings are positioned in the water. In the second, the pylons occupy the extremities of the moles, but Calatrava has seen to it that the protective enclosures rendered necessary when the bridge is open do not occupy significant space. In both cases the technical solution is determinant in the process of connoting the architectural form.

Both versions can be seen as consisting in three parts: the viaducts that link the bridge to the city, the central span, and the mobile elements.

The access viaducts have a structure of reinforced concrete and rise gradually from firm ground to rest upon pylons designed to be thin enough so as not to interfere with the port's seafaring traffic. The reduced dimensions of the footings likewise reduce the amount of work required to build them.

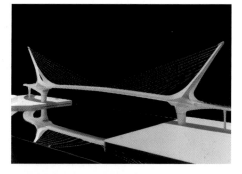

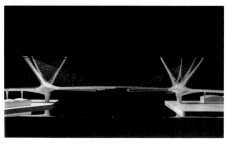

Scale model: suspension swing version

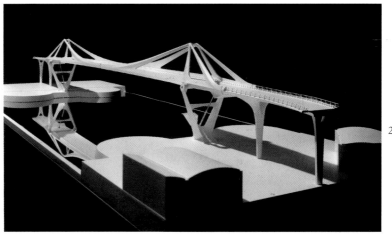

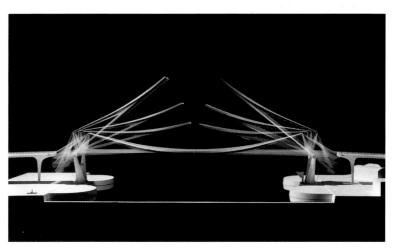

Scale model: bascule version

Piazzale Roma Bridge, Venice, Italy, 1996, project

Footbridge over the Canal Grande
Overall length 88 m
Maximum span 77 m
Height of the arch 7 m

This arch bridge over the Canal Grande connects Piazzale Roma with the Fondamenta di San Lucia, thereby establishing direct communication between the railway station and the parking garage that marks the terminus of the city's automobile access.

The design incorporates for the most part the characteristic features of Venetian bridges, though it differentiates itself from them through certain factors that respond to the necessities of a context that represents a strategic point of convergence of various means of transport.

First of all, the abutments of the bridge are elevated and set back from the edges of the canal so as to avoid interfering in any way with either pedestrian or nautical traffic.

Another important design choice concerns the contiguity of the bridge's longitudinal axis with the facade of the parking garage of Piazzale Roma. This decision was effectuated in anticipation of the eventual construction of an elevated walkway which would run from the apex of the new bridge's arch to the upper levels of the parking garage, thus providing direct access to the bridge from the garage, and vice versa.

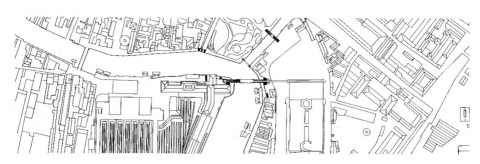

Site plan

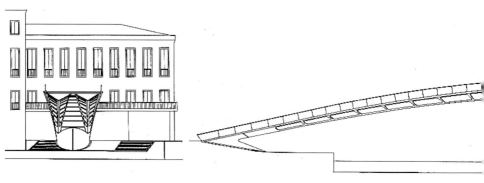

Cross section

Elevation

Scale model

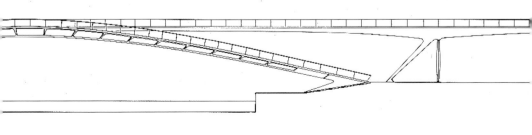

Biography

1951
Santiago Calatrava
Valls is born in
Benimamet, Valencia,
Spain.

1959-1960
Attends the School of Arts
and Trades, Burgasot,
Spain.

1968
Graduates high school,
Valencia.

1968-1969
Attends the Valencia
Academy of Fine Arts.

1969-1974
Studies architecture at the
Escuela Tecnica Superior
de Arquitectura, Valencia.

1975-1979
Studies structural engi-
neering at ETH, Zurich,
Switzerland.

1979-1981
Completes doctorate in
Technical Sciences at
ETH; writes dissertation
on foldable structures;
works as assistant at ETH.

1981
Opens a studio in Zurich.

1985
Sculpture exhibition,
Galérie Jamileh Weber,
Zurich.

1987
Member of BSA
(Federation of Swiss
Architects).
Prix Auguste Perret, UIA
(International Union of
Architects), Paris, France.
Member of the
International Academy of
Architecture.
Participates in the XVII
Triennial, Milan, Italy.

1988
Prize awarded by the City
of Barcelona for the Bach
de Roda bridge.
Prize awarded by the
Asociaciòn de la Prensa,
Valencia.
IABSE Award,
International Association
for Bridge and Structural
Engineering, Hamburg,
Germany.
FAD Prize (Fomento de
las Artes y del Diseno),
Spain.
Fritz Schumacher Prize,
Hamburg.
Member of the Fazlur
Rahman Khan
International Fellowship
for Architecture and
Engineering.

1989
Opens a studio in Paris.
Travelling exhibition, New
York, St. Louis, Chicago,
Los Angeles, Toronto,
Montreal.
Honorary member of the
BDA (Union of German
Architects).

1990
Médaille d'Argent de la
Récherche et de la
Technique, Fondation
Académie d'Architecture,
Paris.

1991
European Glulan Award,
Munich, Germany.
Exhibition, Suomen
Rakennustaiteen Museum,
Helsinki, Finland.
Auszeichnung für gute
Bauten 1991, award from
the City of Zurich for the
Stadelhofen station.
Exhibition, "Dynamische
Gleichgewichte", Design
Museum, Zurich.

1992
Member of the Real

Academia de Bellas Artes
de San Carlos, Valencia.
Member of the Europa
Akademie, Cologne,
Germany.
Exhibition, Dutch
Institute for Architecture,
Rotterdam, The
Netherlands.
Gold Medal Institute of
Structural Engineers,
London, Great Britain.
Brunel Award for the
Stadelhofen station,
Zurich.
Exhibition, Royal Institute
of British Architects,
London.
Exhibition, Arkitktur
Museet, Stockholm,
Sweden.

1993
Exhibition, Deutsches
Museum, Munich.
Exhibition, "Structure
and Expression", Museum
of Modern Art, New
York, USA.
Member of the Royal
Institute of British
Architects, London.
Exhibition, La Llotja,
Valencia.
Exhibition, Overbeck
Gesellschaft, Lubeck,
Germany.
Exhibition, Danish Centre
for Architecture,
Copenhagen, Denmark.
Honorary degree,
Politecnico, Valencia.
Medalla de Honor,
Fomento de la Invenciòn,
Fondaciòn Garcìa
Cabrerizo, Madrid, Spain.
Urban Design Award
from the City of Toronto
for the BCE Place Gallery,
Toronto.

1994
Exhibition, Bruton Street
Gallery, London.
Honorary degree,
University of Seville,

Spain.
Exhibition, Museum of
Applied and Popular Arts,
Moscow, Russia.
Creu de Sant Jordi,
Generalitat de Catalunya,
Barcelona, Spain.
Honorary degree,
University of Edinburgh,
Scotland.
Exhibition, "The
Dynamics of
Equilibrium", Ma Gallery,
Tokyo, Japan.
Exhibition, Arqueria de
los Nuevos Ministerios,
Madrid.
Exhibition, Sala de Arte
La Recova, Santa Cruz de
Tenerife, Spain.
Honorary member, The
Royal Incorporation of
Architects, Great Britain.
Honorary member,
Colegio de Arquitectos,
Mexico City, Mexico.

1995
Exhibition, Belem
Cultural Center, Lisbon,
Portugal.
Exhibition, Galleria
Masieri, Venice, Italy.
Honorary degree,
University College,
Salford, Great Britain.
Award for Good Building
1983-1993, Canton of
Lucerne, Switzerland.

1996
Medalla de Oro al Mérito
de las Bellas Artes,
Ministry of Culture,
Granada, Spain.
Exhibition, Design
Museum, Zurich.
Exhibition, Palazzo della
Ragione, Padua, Italy.
Participates in the
International Exhibition
of Outdoor Sculpture,
Ascona, Switzerland.
Honorary degree,
University of Strathclyde,
Glasgow, Great Britain.

Exhibition, Spazio
Olivetti, Venice.
Exhibition, San Gallo,
Switzerland.
Exhibition, Milwaukee
Art Museum, Milwaukee,
USA.
Exhibition, Britannic
Tower, London.

1997
Honorary degree,
University of Technology,
Delft, The Netherlands.
Exhibition, Israel
National Museum of
Science, Haifa, Israel.
European Award for Steel
Structures, for the recon-
struction of the
Kronprinzen bridge,
Berlin, Germany.
Louis Vuitton-Moet
Hennessy Art Prize, Paris.
Honorary degree,
Milwaukee School of
Engineering, Milwaukee.

1998
Member of Les Arts et
Lettres, Paris.

Essential Bibliography

Santiago Calatrava, exhibition catalogue, Edition Galerie Jamileh Weber, Zurich 1986.

Santiago Calatrava, exhibition catalogue, Generalitat Valenciana, Valencia 1986.

P. Nicolin, *Santiago Calatrava. Il folle volo,* Quaderni di Lotus 7, Electa, Milan 1987.

W. Blaser, *Santiago Calatrava: Ingenieur-Architektur Engineering Architecture,* Birkhäuser Verlag, Basel-Boston-Berlin 1989.

"El Croquis", 38, monographic issue, Madrid 1989

AA.VV., *Ein Bahnhof,* in "Archithése", 2, monographic issue, 1990.

Santiago Calatrava, Dynamische Gleichgewichte: neue Projekte, exhibition catalogue, Artemis Verlag, Zurich 1991.

"El Croquis", 57, monographic issue, Madrid 1992.

R. Harbison, *Creatures from the Mind of the Engineer. The Architecture of Santiago Calatrava,* Artemis Verlag, Zurich 1992.

Santiago Calatrava, D. Sharp, Book Art/E&FN Spon, London 1992.

A.C. Webster, K. Frampton, *Santiago Calatrava,* Schriftenreihe 15, Schule und Museum fur Gestaltung, Zurich 1992.

Santiago Calatrava 1983-93, exhibition catalogue, Valencia 1993, El Croquis Editorial, Madrid 1993.

AA.VV., *Hohe Hauser: kontroverse Beitrage zu einem zu einem umstrittenen Bautypus,* Stuttgart 1993.

K. Frampton, A.C. Webster, A. Tischhauser, *Calatrava Bridges,* Artemis Verlag, Zurich 1993.

B. Klein, *Santiago Calatrava Bahnhof Stadelhofen, Zurich,* Ernst Wasmuth Verlag, Tubingen-Berlin 1993.

M. Mc Quaid, *Santiago Calatrava. Structure and Expression,* exhibition catalogue, Museum of Modern Art, New York 1993.

Santiago Calatrava, The Dynamics of Equilibrium, Ma Gallery, Tokyo 1994.

M.S. Cullen, M. Kieren, *Calatrava Berlin Five Projects,* Birkhäuser Verlag, Basel-Boston-Berlin 1994.

M. Le Roux e M. Rivoire, *Calatrava Escale Satolas,* Editions Glénat, Grenoble 1994.

A. Tzonis, L. Lefaivre, *Movement, Structure and the Work of Santiago Calatrava,* Birkhäuser Verlag, Basel-Boston-Berlin 1995.

M. Zardini, *Santiago*

Calatrava. Libro segreto, F. Motta, Milano 1995.

Santiago Calatrava, 1983-1996 in "AV. Monografias", 61, monographic issue, Madrid 1996.

S. Polano, *Santiago Calatrava,* "Documenti di Architettura", Electa, Milan 1996.

A. Tischauser, S. von Moss, *Public Buildings,* Birkhäuser Verlag, Basel-Boston-Berlin 1998.

Projects and completed works

Acleta Bridge, Disentis, Switzerland, 1979, project

IBA Squash Hall, Berlin, Germany, 1979, competition, project

Exposition Hall, Züspa, Zurich, Switzerland, 1981, competition

Letten Bridge, Zurich, Switzerland, 1982, competition, project

Schwarzhaupt Factory, Dielsdorf, Switzerland, 1982, competition, project

Mühlenareal Library, Thun, Switzerland, 1982, competition, project

Bridge over the Rhine, Diepoldsau, Switzerland, 1982, competition, project

Exterior remodelling of the Thalberg House, Zurich, Switzerland, 1983, built

Baumwollhof Balcony, Zurich, Switzerland, 1983, built

Jakem Factory, Munchwilen, Switzerland, 1983-1984, built

Ernstings Factory, Coesfeld, Germany, 1983-1985, competition, built

Roof for a Post Office, Lucerne, Switzerland, 1983-1985, built

Bus Stop, St. Fiden, San Gallo, Switzerland, 1983-1985, built

Cantonal School, Wohlen, Switzerland, 1984-1988, built

Station Hall, Lucerne, Switzerland, 1983-1989, built

Stadelhofen Train Station, Zurich, Switzerland, 1983-1990, competition, built

Concert Hall, Bärenmatte Community Center, Suhr, Switzerland, 1983-1988, built

De Sede Exposition Pavilion, Zurich, Switzerland, 1984, competition, built

Caballeros Bridge, Lerida, Spain, 1984, competition, project

Dobi Office Complex, Suhr, Switzerland, 1984-1985, built

Felipe II – Bach de Roda Bridge, Barcelona, Spain, 1984-1987, built

Feldenmoos Park and Footbridge, Feldenmoos, Switzerland, 1985, competition, project

Traffic Signage along Avenida Diagonal, Barcelona, Spain, 1986, built

Concert Hall for a Music School, San Gallo, Switzerland, 1986, built

Raitenau Overpass, Salzburg, Austria, 1986, competition, project

Blackbox Television Studio, Zurich, Switzerland, 1986-1987, built

Cabaret Tabourettli, Basel, Switzerland, 1986-1987, built

9 de Octubre Bridge, Valencia, Spain, 1986-1989, built

Footbridge, Thiers, France, 1987, project

Bridge, Pontevedra, Spain, 1987, project

Basarrate Subway Station, Bilbao, Spain, 1987, competition, project

Exterior Bank, Zurich, Switzerland, 1987, built

Cascine Bridge, Florence, Italy, 1987, project

Oudry-Mesly Footbridge, Créteil-Paris, France, 1987-1988, built

BCE Place Gallery, Toronto, Canada, 1987-1992, built

Alamillo Bridge, Seville, Spain, 1987-1992, built

PCW Housing Complex, Würenlingen, Switzerland, 1987-1996, built

Prè Babel Sports Center, Geneva, Switzerland, 1988, project

Leimbach Footbridge, Zurich, Switzerland, 1988, competition, project

Collserola Telecommunications Tower, Barcelona, Spain, 1988, competition, project

Wettstein Bridge, Basel, Switzerland, 1988, project

Gentil Bridge, Paris, France, 1988, competition, project

Bauschänzli Restaurant,

Zurich, Switzerland, 1988, project

Emergency Services Center, San Gallo, Switzerland, 1988, under construction

Lusitania Bridge, Merida, Spain, 1988-1991, built

Miraflores Bridge, Cordoba, Spain, 1989, project

219

Canopy for a Bus and a Tram Stop, Zurich, Switzerland, 1989, project

Reuss Footbridge, Fluelen, Switzerland, 1989, competition, project

Law Library, University of Zurich, Switzerland, 1989, not built

Muri Monastery, Canton d'Argovia, Switzerland, 1989, project

Swissbau Pavilion, Basel, Switzerland, 1989, built

Floating Pavilion, Lake Lucerne, Switzerland, 1989, project

Gran Via Bridge, Barcelona, 1989, competition, project

Port de la Lune Swing Bridge, Bordeaux, France, 1989, project

La Devesa Bridge, Ripoll, 1989-1991, built

Montjuic Tower, Barcelona, Spain, 1989-1992, built

Rhône-Alpes TGV Station, Satolas, Lyon, France,

1989-1994, competition, built

Puerto Bridge, Ondarroa, Spain, 1989-1995, built

Canopy for a Bus Stop, San Gallo, Switzerland, 1989-1996, built

Spitalfields Gallery, London, Great Britain, 1990, project

East London Crossing, London, Great Britain, 1990, project

Nuovo ponte sul Vecchio, Corsica, France, 1990, competition, project

Belluard Theatre, Fribourg, Switzerland, 1990, project

Sondica Airport, Bilbao, Spain, 1990, under construction

Campo Volantin footbridge, Bilbao, Spain, 1990-1997, built

Auditorium, Santa Cruz de Tenerife, Spain, 1991, not built

Médoc Bridge, Bordeaux, France, 1991, invitational competition, project

Football Stadium, Reggio Calabria, Italy, 1991, competition, project

Telecommunications tower, Valencia, Spain, 1991, project

Football Stadium, Salou, Spain, 1991, competition, project

"City of Science" Cultural Complex, Valencia, Spain,

1991, competition, under construction

Highway Bridge, Lille, France, 1991, competition, project

Cathedral of St. John the Divine, New York, USA, 1991, invitational competition, project

Beton Forum Standard Bridge, Stockholm, Sweden, 1991, project

Spandau Train Station, Berlin, Germany, 1991, invitational competition, project

Railroad Bridge, Klosterstrasse, Berlin, Germany, 1991, project

Kuwait Pavilion, Seville, Spain, 1991-1992, built and dismantled

Bridge and Subway Station, Alameda, Valencia, Spain, 1991-1995, competition, built

Kronprinzen Bridge, Berlin, Germany, 1991-1996, competition, built

Completion of the Oberbaum Bridge, Berlin, Germany, 1991-1996, built

Jahn Sportpark, Berlin, Germany, 1992, invitational competition, project

Solferino Bridge, Paris, France, 1992, project

Modular Subway Station, London, Great Britain, 1992, project

Renovation and expansion of the Reichstag, Berlin,

Germany, 1992, invitational competition, project

Serreria Bridge, Valencia, Spain, 1992, project

Bridge, Lucerne, Switzerland, 1992, competition, project

Bridge, Alcoy, Spain, 1992, project

Shadow Machine, sculpture, New York, USA, 1992-1993, built

Exposition Center, Santa Cruz de Tenerife, Spain, 1992-1995, built

Municipal Hall and redesign of Plaza España, Alcoy, Spain, 1992-1995, built

Öresund Bridge, Copenhagen, Denmark, 1993, competition, project

Ile Falcon Bridge, Sierre, Switzerland, 1993 competition, project

Granadilla Bridge, Tenerife, Spain, 1993, competition, project

Telecommunications Tower, Alicante, Spain, 1993, project

Bridge, Murcia, Spain, 1993, project

Southpoint Pavilion, New York, USA, 1993, project

Trinity Bridge, Salford, Manchester, Great Britain, 1993-1995, built

Control Tower, Sondica Airport, Bilbao, Spain,

1993-1996, competition, built

Oriente Station, Lisbon, Portugal, 1993-1998, competition, built

St. Paul's Bridge, London, Great Britain, 1994, project

Manrique Footbridge, Murcia, Spain, 1994, project

Quay Point Bridge, Bristol, Great Britain, 1994, project

Milwaukee Art Museum, Milwaukee, USA, 1994, under construction

Convention Center, Fiuggi, Italy, 1994, under construction

Football Stadium, Marseilles, France, 1995, competition, project

Turtle Bay Footbridge, Redding, USA, 1995, project

Roof for the Central Station, Zurich, Switzerland, 1995, invitational competition, project

Poole Harbour Bridge, Portsmouth, Great Britain, 1995, competition, project

Footbridge, Bedford, Great Britain, 1995, competition, project

Sundsvall Bridge, Sundsvall, Sweden, 1995, competition, project

Stadium, Bilbao, Spain, 1995, project

Piazzale Roma Bridge,

Venice, Italy, 1996,
competition, project

Olympia Stadium,
Stockholm, Sweden, 1996,
competition, project

Church of the Year 2000,
Rome, Italy, 1996,
competition, project

Chapel of the Tomb of
Brother Junipero, Los
Angeles, USA, 1996,
invitational competition,
project

City Point Tower, London,
Great Britain, 1996,
project

Mimico Creek footbridge,
Toronto, Canada, 1996,
project

Arts Center, Valencia,
Spain, 1996, under
construction

Service Station, Geneva,
Switzerland, 1996,
competition, under
construction

TGV Station, Lieges,
Belgium, 1996,
competition, under
construction

Bridge, Orleans, France,
1996, competition, under
construction

Port of Barcelona,
Barcelona, Spain, 1997,
competition, project

Barajas Airport, Madrid,
Spain, 1997, competition,
project

Cultural Center, San Gallo,
Switzerland, 1997, under
construction

Pennsylvania Station, New

York, USA, 1998,
competition, project

Petach-Tikva footbridge,
Tel Aviv, Israel, 1998, not
built

Photograph Credits

Sergio Belinchon:
p. 9; 154; 154-155; 156;
157

Alessandra Chemollo:
p. 215

Studio Calatrava:
p. 10; 15

Heinrich Helfenstein:
p. 10; 39; 49; 50; 56; 62; 68;
71; 72; 73; 75; 78; 79; 81;
86; 88; 89; 90; 91; 92; 93;
98; 99; 101; 102; 103; 104;
105; 107; 110; 111; 113;
114; 121; 123; 125; 134;
135; 136; 143; 144; 145;
147; 148; 149; 151; 152;
153; 160; 161; 170; 171;
176; 177; 179; 180; 186;
195; 196; 201; 203; 206;
210; 211; 212; 213

Paolo Rosselli:
p. 10; 12; 17; 18; 19; 21;
22; 23; 24; 25; 26; 27; 28;
29; 30; 31; 32; 33; 34; 35;
36; 37; 39; 40; 41; 42; 43;
44; 45; 52; 53; 54; 55; 57;
58; 60; 61; 62; 63; 65; 66;
67; 82; 83; 84; 85; 95; 96;
97; 115; 116; 117; 118;
119; 128/129; 130; 131;
137; 138; 139; 140; 141;
163; 164; 165; 166; 167;
168/169; 172; 173; 174;
175; 181; 182/183; 184;
185; 187; 188; 189; 190;
191; 192/193; 197; 198;
199; 207; 208; 209